LOST AND FOUND

From Racecar Driver to Pilgrim,
from Soweto to Findhorn

LOST AND FOUND

From Racecar Driver to Pilgrim,
from Soweto to Findhorn

GEOFF DALGLISH

FINDHORN PRESS

Published in 2012 by Findhorn Press, Scotland

ISBN 978-1-84409-597-9

Edited by Michael Hawkins
Cover design by Richard Crookes
Interior design by Damian Keenan
Photo credits see p. 187
Printed and bound in the EU

1 2 3 4 5 6 7 8 9 17 16 15 14 13 12

CONTENTS

DEDICATION

For Tammy and Bonnie and all Gaia Earth's children.

And to the Findhorn Foundation community that inspires me and is a sheltering tree when I know not where my footsteps will lead me.

INTRODUCTION

THE SECRET

If at first, the idea is not absurd, then there is no hope for it.
— *ALBERT EINSTEIN*, PHYSICIST

Hey, whatever happened to the party animal and wild child? Where is the prankster who insisted that if you weren't living on the edge, you were wasting space? Or the speed merchant and power addict who regularly risked jail by driving at more than 240 km/h on public roads? Or the serial womaniser who even cheated on his mistresses? Or the journalist who faced death at the hands of an angry mob during the June 1976 *apartheid* uprising in Soweto, South Africa's largest and most infamous black township? Or the photographer who coolly suppressed his horror while stepping over charred human remains to capture haunting images of the still-smouldering wreckage of a civilian airliner downed by a terrorist missile?

Fast forward a few years and we find him not at the wheel of a fast car but quietly living the simple life in Findhorn, a remote but celebrated ecovillage and spiritual community in Scotland that has been described as a beacon of light in a troubled world.

According to myth and legend it is a place of transformation and inspiration where many live joyfully in love and absolute faith.

Whoa Bess! Has our fun-loving petrolhead fallen into a black hole?

Instead of a turbocharged, high-octane diet of speed and thrills, we find that his life has slowed to walking pace in a community that grows organic vegetables, fashions funky wooden homes from recycled materials including whisky barrels, and generates its own electricity with whirring wind turbines and solar panels.

Welcome to the Findhorn Foundation, a home to around 500 committed souls who have grabbed the headlines over the years by talking to plants and creating a community with one of the lowest recorded ecological footprints in the developed world. Welcome to a simpler, gentler way of living which emphasises the well-being of the planet and all its inhabitants above ego and personal enrichment. And surprise,

surprise – instead of an atmosphere of sacrifice and deprivation, we find joy and fulfil-ment. And it's catching.

My days, weeks and months of meditation, walking in nature, and begging God for guidance and inspiration have finally paid off. She's been listening – bless Her! I feel like a lottery winner: exhilarated and dazzled at my good fortune! At the ripe age of 60-something I've hit the jackpot and definitely will not be retiring with newspaper, slippers and rocker in front of the fire.

Quite the reverse, in fact, and I'm breathless with excitement at the prospect. Suddenly I know what I've been born into this lifetime for and realize how I can truly make a difference. I will *'be the change I wish to see in the world,'* taking my cue from Mahatma Gandhi who also insisted that *'the best way to find yourself is to lose yourself in the service of others.'*

Looking back I see now how each chapter in my story has been another step along the path, preparing me for this day when I would be ready to fulfil my unique destiny, boldly embracing radical change and stepping forward at last to play my role in the world.

―――――――

It is hard to pinpoint exactly when and where the glimmerings of the idea started, certainly many years earlier, and perhaps under the stars in the Central American jungles of Guatemala during the annual Camel Trophy 4x4 torture-fest of 1995.

Lying on my back and gazing at a night sky dazzling in its enormity and inten-sity, I suddenly knew my life could never be the same. I'd never again be satisfied with only the outer trappings of success – my prized editorship; a double storey home on five acres and a luxury 4x4 in the garage. Even a loving wife and two amazing daughters weren't enough – there had to be more.

And I'd found it.

My secret grew inside me, nourished by a sense of purpose and certainty: a life-long rollercoaster of fun and adventure had been preparing me for this moment. I'd let go of fear – and especially a fear of failure – and take a huge leap of faith.

I'd had my epiphany while staying at Findhorn during 2010 and back home in South Africa I couldn't wait to tell my daughters Bonnie and Tammy; eagerly anticipating their reaction … astonishment perhaps, approval hopefully.

"I've decided on some major life changes," I announced rather pompously, "and feel I have found a way to make a difference while raising awareness around some important spiritual and environmental issues."

Tammy, Bonnie, Geoff and a tree friend

Taking a deep breath, I prepared to launch into my plans when Tammy, the youngest, who is well known for her incisive wit and often biting sarcasm, interrupted. "Dad, you want to walk the world," she declared, straight-faced and serious.

I was stunned, demanding to know how she'd stumbled onto the truth. What had sparked that flash of intuition? "I just knew," she said. "And I knew you'd want to do something big to get your message across."

Wow!

Bonnie, my equally idealistic first-born, was matter-of-fact, asking penetrating and practical questions about where, when and why.

My idea, after a much envied life of fast cars and jet-set travel, was to morph from petrolhead to pilgrim, shedding worldly possessions and walking with a message about treading lightly and lovingly upon the Earth. It would be an inner journey as much as an outer one that would probably amaze and delight some friends, appalling others who'd be convinced I'd finally lost the plot.

It felt great … wild, scary, daunting but irresistible and totally liberating. I'd step into the future as Earth Pilgrim Africa, a simple and virtually penniless seeker and messenger.

CHAPTER ONE

IN THE BEGINNING

The true meaning of life is to plant trees,
under whose shade you do not expect to sit.
— *NELSON HENDERSON,* PIONEER FARMER

"Tees, tees!" I exclaimed excitedly from my lofty perch astride my father's shoulders as he strolled through the local park with my mother.

At first they were mildly taken aback: surprise at my first ever words turning to delight at the realization that I was saying 'trees.'

I have a fuzzy memory of that and similar days and the sense of wonder at being surrounded by so many huge trees. I guess those early outings helped set the scene for a lifelong love affair with nature and all creatures, something that I shared with both my parents.

Too many times as a little boy I'd wake up sobbing when I discovered the bug I'd clutched tightly in my hand throughout the night had suffocated. They were my little friends and I definitely meant them no harm!

Other pals included almost everything that hopped, slithered, swam and flew. I surfed or snorkelled in the warm Indian Ocean every day before school and couldn't get home fast enough to rip off shoes and school uniform and race back to the beach or to explore the nearby bush. Sometimes I'd catch snakes, being careful not to harm them, and invariably I'd spend long hours watching birds and learning their habits.

From the local Africans I discovered that flying ants, a kind of termite that swarmed immediately after the summer rains, could be caught in their hundreds and thousands and fried in a pan. I delighted in watching swallows and other birds grabbing the mid-air snacks on the wing.

My mother, meanwhile, was expressing her fascination for the wilds in a series of animal stories for children published in our local Durban newspaper, *The Natal Mercury*. Later a compilation appeared in book form as *Tales from the Baobab Tree*.

It is dedicated to 'Geoffrey, Donald, Marion and all South Africa's children.' What a tribute from a loving Mum and one that I pass on to my own offspring with this book: 'For Tammy and Bonnie and all Gaia Earth's children.'

Geoff with his mum who instilled a great love of nature

Dad's passion was regular holiday motoring trips to game reserves and conservation areas in the Zululand bushveld and Drakensberg Mountains of Kwa-Zulu Natal, or his absolute favourite, the Kruger National Park, South Africa's premier wildlife sanctuary which is today part of the pioneering Great Limpopo Transfrontier Park shared with neighbouring countries Mozambique and Zimbabwe.

Kruger remains one of Africa's great conservation icons, although it seemed much wilder then, Dad having to stop every so often on the way there to cool the car's engine when it threatened to overheat; while once we arrived, there were few tourists and vast tracts of wilderness accessed exclusively by dirt roads.

It was – and is – a magical place that is home to the Big Five: elephant, rhino, buffalo, lion and leopard and many endangered creatures driven to extinction elsewhere by humanity's greed and thoughtlessness.

An early memory is of a dramatic charge by a huge bull elephant, viewed through the back window of the car as my father frantically U-turned and then accelerated down a bumpy sand track with the ear-flapping giant in hot pursuit. They can run at 40 km/h and to a little boy that seemed very fast indeed, but possibly more thrilling than frightening. My Dad the Hero took care of things as I knew he would!

Rivalling the charge as the highlight of that holiday was witnessing the tables being turned on a pride of lions hiding out in a thicket near a waterhole. Several times a herd of hundreds of thirsty wildebeest and antelope attempted to reach the water's edge, only to thunder off panic-stricken when confronted by young lionesses learning to hunt.

Finally a magnificent sable antelope with curving scimitar horns appeared on the scene and calmly began walking towards the waterhole despite the threatening presence of the pride. The inevitable happened and as the sable took flight a lioness leapt onto the huge antelope's back, only to have it throw back its head, the razor-sharp horns severely goring the surprised young predator.

The lioness limped away, bleeding profusely, while the sable confidently headed back to the waterhole like a Pied Piper of the Bushveld, this time with all the other animals following. It was a remarkable sight, the likes of which I've never seen since.

As a young boy I visited the Durban public library and adjoining museum each week with the same sense of excitement and wonder, taking out my maximum allocation of nature books and spending hours studying the exhibits.

Perhaps more than any other book it was *Serengeti Shall not Die* that kindled my passion to become a game ranger and guardian of the wild creatures of the Earth.

Written by German biologist and director of the Frankfurt Zoological Society Bernhard Grzimek, it is the remarkable story of a father and son's love affair with Africa and their courage and determination in seeking conservation status for Ngorongoro Crater and neighbouring Serengeti, scene of the annual migration that has been described as The Greatest Show on Earth.

Virtually simultaneous with the release of the book was the film of the same name, memorializing handsome young Michael Grzimek who died in a flying accident on location during the filming. He was just 24 when his zebra-striped aircraft collided with a vulture on takeoff.

It won the Academy Award for the best documentary film in 1959 and resonated around the world to tremendous public acclaim, succeeding spectacularly in raising conservation awareness and establishing the Serengeti as one of the world's unspoilt wildlife gems.

I was mesmerized and wanted nothing more than to be like that formidable and inspiring father and son team.

In recent years I visited their legacy no fewer than eight times in 10 years.

No, I didn't become a game ranger, although I've worked on a number of conservation projects, raised funds and awareness and had the satisfaction of sharing so many wildlife experiences with my writings and photography.

In the 1970s I participated in a crocodile rescue operation at Lake St Lucia, which is today part of iSimangaliso, South Africa's first world heritage site. I gave myself one of the biggest frights of my life when I fell out of a boat and onto a crocodile we were attempting to drag to the shore with a rope.

Later I worked as many weekends as I could at the country's first cheetah sanctuary, getting to know these speedsters of the animal kingdom intimately and always being moved by their magnificence and vulnerability, especially at the hands of farmers who hunted them. When we offered to pay for any livestock killed by the spotted predators there were no takers, one hunter even bragging that he'd killed two of these endangered creatures with a single bullet. Trophies were more prized than the occasional sheep that became a cheetah dinner, rather than lamb chops on the barbecue!

Geoff with cheetah at the pioneering South African sanctuary

In 2004 I played a behind-the-scenes role in supporting Africa MegaFlyover, a massive international conservation project aimed at identifying and saving the continent's wilderness treasures. It had the inspirational leadership of Mike Fay, National Geographic's explorer-at-large who taught me that one person can indeed make a difference.

I was stunned and delighted to be named an honorary member of The Bateleurs, an environmental air force comprising volunteer pilots who champion protection of the Earth's delicate ecosystems. The non-profit, non-governmental organisation, which is the African equivalent of America's LightHawk volunteer fliers, takes its name from one of Africa's most magnificent eagles and does wonderful work.

I felt that at last I was making a meaningful difference and was beginning to glimpse the way ahead.

CHAPTER TWO

SEEING THE LIGHT

To fall in love with God is the greatest of all romances;
to seek him, the greatest adventure:
to find him, the greatest human achievement.
— *RAPHAEL SIMON*, AUTHOR

Who can say when we have our first conscious glimmerings of the spiritual beings we are? My awakenings certainly started very young and were mostly fed by the diet of Christian teachings I was dished up at school and my local churches, which projected the image of an angry, vengeful, needy and neurotic God with strangely human traits.

Somehow that never rang true, although for a while I read my Bible religiously, reminding myself that *"A chapter a day, keeps the devil away!"*

By the time I was around 10-years-old I was sneaking out of school during lunch-break to a nearby home for prayer meetings where we kneeled on the floor and appealed loudly to the Almighty to forgive our many sins. How could a small boy with a passionate love of all life be so wicked that he faced burning in the everlasting fires?

I was uncomfortable with all the ranting, hoping the noise wouldn't carry across to the school. But I did feel good when I was hugged and praised and told that I had been *saved* by Jesus Christ, who loved me and promised I would go to heaven.

What a relief! Hell and Purgatory didn't sound like much fun and my salvation was a giddy moment to eclipse even getting a new badge in the Boy Scouts.

Looking back I realise that the Scouting movement, of which my father was a leading light, did more for me than all the fear-based church teachings, encouraging my great love of the outdoors, nature and camping.

Ironically one of my first moments of great doubt arrived unexpectedly one bright Sunday morning when my beloved new Raleigh sports bicycle, with its thumb-operated three-speed gearshift, was stolen. I had propped it up against the wall of the local Methodist church while inside singing hymns joyfully and having the honour of reading to the congregation from the scriptures. It was a New Testament favourite from St John, Chapter 14: *"In my Father's house there are many mansions ... "*

How could God have allowed this to happen when I was faithfully following the path? It was a time of disillusionment and questioning.

Later, when my family moved to Tokyo and it was feared that there would be no suitable English-language education in Japan, I enrolled at Kearsney College, one of South Africa's leading schools which has a strong Christian and Methodist ethos, although it welcomes boys of all faiths.

My first big lesson at boarding school was that if I didn't stand up for myself I'd be victimized by my peers, so when one of the biggest and toughest bullies decided to pick on me before morning inspection, I knew exactly what I had to do : humiliate him and send out the message that I was not to be messed with.

I exploded into action, remembering all my father's martial arts' teachings, and used the bigger boy's momentum to hurl him to the ground and then knock him down every time he tried to get up; finally dragging him around the floor until his smart Kearsney uniform was smeared with red floor polish. I was fast and agile, making up for what I lacked in size and strength. He was a demoralised mess.

I'd arrived and gained instant respect, becoming one of a rebellious 'elite' who showed a disdain for authority and regulations. My classmates regularly covered for me when I bunked out from daily devotions in the Chapel, a beautiful old building I'd love to revisit someday.

Things came to a head when our little group crammed into a tiny Morris Minor one night that had been 'borrowed' from a friend; and then drove illegally a few miles to a private party we gate-crashed. We were all too young to have a driver's licence and were well aware that the school had sounded an ominous warning: discipline would be strictly enforced and anybody going absent without leave would be expelled.

Sauntering into the party I was shocked to see my much-loved collie dog, Rusty, standing in the doorway and looking mournfully at me. Out of all the homes and parties we could have picked, we'd chosen the one that belonged to the kindly people my parents had given my dog to when they left for Japan. I was shattered and backed out of the house, fighting back tears. My party ended before it began.

The drama and heartache of the night was not over, though.

Returning to school we discovered that one of us had left a dormitory light on and when the housemaster investigated, he discovered a number of his young charges were missing. We were caught red-handed trying to sneak back in!

"Were you smoking?" the principal later demanded when I sat nervously in his office. "No Sir," I lied, and simultaneously we both noticed nicotine-stains on two fingers of my right hand. Could it get worse than this?

A call to my father followed and the headmaster petulantly announced: "Your son lacks parental control," stating the obvious. "Of course, he does," my father retorted. "That's why he's with you." I was very proud of my Dad's support and even less enamoured with the restrictions of school; despite the fact that an earlier decision to expel me was reversed.

I felt like a prisoner, robbed of all my freedoms. One of my greatest joys had been to go walkabout and roam freely in nature, studying the birds and tiniest creatures. Now I wasn't allowed off campus other than during approved group excursions like sporting matches to other schools. And nothing encapsulated my loss of freedom more than the compulsory devotional sessions in the Chapel each evening.

Anger and resentment boiled over and I found myself silently mouthing the challenge: "If there really is a God: show me! Prove that you exist."

What followed was a few seconds that changed my life forever and crushed all doubts.

Predictably I was sitting in the back row and was suddenly engulfed and over-whelmed by the most dazzling light-show to the accompaniment of exquisite ce-lestial music. The cross, with the tortured figure of Christ nailed to it, rose off the far wall beyond the pulpit and floated towards me until it was close enough to touch. All awareness of everything else disappeared and my entire universe was made up of the crucifix and lights, colours and sounds that defy description. They were unlike anything I'd experienced before or since and I have no words to de-scribe the *feelings* of euphoria I felt.

It was utterly life-changing and my first incomparable taste of utter bliss and oneness with the love, joy, peace and power of divine energy. God had reached out and touched me.

CHAPTER THREE

THE POWER OF LOVE

Love is something eternal;
the aspect may change, but not the essence …
— *VINCENT VAN GOGH*, PAINTER

For this idealistic young reporter there was no place on Earth more exciting or relevant in the 1970s than the newsroom of the *Rand Daily Mail*, a world-renowned Johannesburg daily newspaper characterised by a crusading anti-*apartheid* stance.

On a big news day the atmosphere was electric; typewriters clacking away noisily, reporters yelling into telephones and the news editor demanding updates almost before reporters had sat down at their desks in untidy rows in the bustling open-plan office.

It was a dream come true as I found myself living the fantasy and being part of the big story, be it a civil uprising, an air disaster, or perhaps the death in detention of a political detainee whose only crime was to oppose State-sponsored violence and racial discrimination.

I have amazing memories of that newsroom, but the most vivid is of the delectable Scottish lass who always seemed to be moving too swiftly past my desk; serene, purposeful and propelled by some inner joy. She was quite the most gorgeous thing imaginable and almost 40 years later I can still picture her then in my mind's eye.

Carol McMillan Lochhead was the news editor's able secretary and I remember a photographer wistfully announcing: "She's the one I'm going to marry!" Wrong, I thought. Get to the back of the queue. Not that marriage featured on my priority list, although getting to know this delectable blonde creature definitely did.

My hero then was a veteran reporter called Bob Hitchcock, who'd covered wars and lived on the pavement with squatters. He and his wonderful wife Gloria were like adopted parents to Carol and it became a game that they first had to OK my formal requests for dates, pretending to deliberate at length, although they were secretly in favour of the blossoming romance.

When kittens were born at my home I had a better come-on line than 'Come and see my etchings.' Carol visited and soon we were a cuddly family, all rejoicing in each other's company.

It was one great adventure and three years later, in 1976, I felt like a teenage runaway when we chose to get married while on holiday in the UK, obtaining a special licence signed by the Archbishop of Canterbury in an office called The Sanctuary alongside London's Houses of Parliament.

An exiled bishop, who I'd interviewed when he was kicked out of Namibia because of his inclusive views on parishioners of all colours, assured me: "I have just the church for you, across the village green in Sutton Courtenay."

He was right. It is an idyllic 12th Century church and the ceremony was inspir-

Carol during her days as the fashion editor for the Sunday Times

ing, our respective best friends there to witness our day of joy while family unfortunately had to rely on a phone call for the glad tidings.

Afterwards the minister rang the church bells enthusiastically and unknown to us, that was a signal to the villagers to celebrate with us in the adjoining pub. Their friendship and generosity was overwhelming and it turned out to be a free wedding reception – I don't think we paid for a single drink.

Happy days... Geoff, Carol and a licence to marry in 1976

Life seemed sublime then, although we were to discover a greater joy when we two became three and then four.

If love is something you learn, then Bonnie and Tammy are our greatest teachers and bestowed the gift of unconditional love so freely given and received.

I recall the sense of wonder at tiny little hands grasping a finger, or arms wrapped limpet-like around my neck and countless evenings when they'd announce: "Dad, it is sleep time," which was a summons regardless of what I might be busy with. I'd make up stories and invariably fall asleep with them, sometimes only waking hours later, before crawling in with Carol.

She was the night owl and I the early bird, so the routines worked perfectly with me getting them up and delivering them to school, having made their sandwiches.

Perhaps the worst day in my life was in 1996, when we'd been together 23 years and married almost 20 of those. I'd met somebody else and decided to leave home.

We sat Tammy and Bonnie down in the lounge and delivered the bombshell. Bon, the oldest at 15, went very, very quiet, while Tam, a vulnerable 13-year-old was devastated and disbelieving: "But you don't fight or anything," she lamented, trying to make sense of it, before running to her room sobbing.

It felt like the worst kind of betrayal and haunted me for years after, with Tammy initially putting a wall between us. Are you trying to punish me, I asked? "You better believe it," she said, and I think the turning point only came about three years later when she and I had a holiday together in Zimbabwe, canoeing the mighty Zambezi River and camping out in lion and elephant country. Nature helped heal our hurts.

The thawing was incremental and has been a lesson in the power of love, demonstrating again and again that there is nothing in the world more persuasive and compelling than the love that is at the core of our being.

In recent years we've shared a number of great adventures, a highlight being a self-guided Tanzanian camping trip with the girls that included Ngorongoro Crater and the Serengeti Game Reserve, where we were pinned down by lions mating outside the tent.

Perhaps the proudest time was when Carol and I swapped jokes and reminiscences in the back of the car, while Bonnie and Tammy chauffeured us on the long drive to Tam's wedding to a lovely young man, Grant Lapping.

"We've done well," Carol mused, voicing thanks for all our many blessings.

I feel that same gratitude every day when I have my early morning meditative walk and consciously count my good fortune, always starting with the gift that Carol and I share of two wonderful daughters.

Tammy on her wedding day

The last time I hugged them both was when I began my walking pilgrimage on the sacred Isle of Iona on July 7, 2011, and it will probably always be one of my most poignant memories.

I was so touched that they both flew to the Findhorn community, where I'd been staying, and chose to spend a few days with me before I set off.

Who knows where or when we'll next meet, although I'm greatly comforted by a message I read on a tombstone while camping in a cemetery: "Your loved ones are only a thought away." I think of them a lot.

Bonnie and Tammy growing up

CHAPTER FOUR

THEY'RE GOING TO KILL YOU!

There is no easy walk to freedom anywhere, and many of us
will have to pass through the valley of the shadow of death again
and again before we reach the mountaintop of our desires.

— *NELSON MANDELA,* FORMER SOUTH AFRICAN PRESIDENT
AND ROBBEN ISLAND PRISONER

"Get out quick; they're going to kill you!" The front-page headline in a yellowing press clipping from the *Rand Daily Mail* of June 1976 shouts the story of the dark days when the giant black township of Soweto erupted and there were running battles in the streets between heavily-armed police and protesting schoolchildren.

On June 16 black outrage at an unfair education system that discriminated ruthlessly against children of colour, finally spilled over, intensifying the struggle that would one day see former prisoner Nelson Mandela taking his rightful place at the head of a society that is a celebration of democratic principles.

If one day can change the course of a nation's history, then this was the day as unrest spread like a wildfire across South Africa and sealed the fate of the brutal *apartheid* regime. Sadly more than 600 people, many of them children, were to die in the bloodbath before the year was out.

That first day also claimed the lives of two white officials, one of them Dr Melville Edelstein, a compassionate sociologist who had devoted his life to the upliftment of the black community. He was stoned to death by a crazed mob and left with a sign around his neck proclaiming: 'Beware Afrikaaners'.

Like so many South Africans that night my wife Carol and I tried to make sense of the madness and horror. She had met and liked Dr Edelstein while doing charity work in the township, where she helped distribute blankets to the poor and needy at the outset of winter.

It was also on that dramatic first day of the uprising that one of the most famous images of the 20th century was snapped. Think of the Vietnam War and you'll probably picture a naked young girl fleeing from a napalm attack, while the cruelty of *apartheid* is personified by a photograph of a dying schoolboy being carried in the arms of a caring stranger.

Thirteen-year-old Hector Pieterson had been shot by the police moments before, and all the horror of the moment is captured forever in the haunting photograph as his 16-year-old sister Antoinette, runs alongside, screaming hysterically.

Mrs Antoinette Sithole and the famous photograph in
which she runs alongside her dying brother Hector

Although Hector was not the first to die that day, the power of that photograph made him a symbol of the liberation struggle. Today the memorial to the Soweto schoolchildren's uprising bears his name, as does the adjoining museum.

Hours after that first explosion of violence I was on the scene, my brief as a young photo-journalist being to capture the emotions of a people torn apart by the unrest. Drama soon reared its head at Baragwanath Hospital, the largest in Africa which has since been renamed the Chris Hani Memorial Hospital.

Ugly scenes of violence threatened to spread to the black nursing staff when armed police refused to admit a 14-year-old schoolboy who had been shot three times.

Angry hospital staff, most of them women in their starched white uniforms, surged forward shouting their protest while the car carrying the injured boy was delayed at the hospital gates by police of the special anti-riot squad.

For a few frightening moments the crowd's outrage was directed at me, a lone white face in a sea of black anger. "Let him in; this is a hospital," they demanded while I was jostled and roughly handled.

I yelled at the officials to open up and a couple of minutes later the car was waved through, although all hospital beds were apparently already full. The child, Patrick Rakau, was wheeled away on a stretcher. He had been shot on the playing field of a nearby school.

Moments later another injured child arrived and I was ordered off the premises by a hospital official. "No Press. No photographs," I was told.

Outside the hospital gates a gauntlet of flying rocks and missiles lay ahead.

My first sight was a man dripping blood and moaning. He had been hit in the face by a rock the size of a fist.

Nearby a truck had crashed into a wall after being hit by missiles hurled only metres away from the hospital.

A black motorist shouted through his window: "Get out quick. They are going to kill you."

Similar warnings were sounded again and again. A white face was like a red flag to a bull all along the interminable four kilometres to safety.

Twice I had to race through a mob of jeering faces and flying rocks.

Up ahead I saw all the side windows of a small car smashed, while an expensive sports car had its windscreen shattered.

Many black faces registered the same terror as the whites, and one black motorist swerved off the road and careered through the veldt. He didn't realise that a fist clenched in a Black Power salute would have guaranteed him safe passage through an unofficial roadblock.

Rioters stoned and looted a truck which ironically was carrying beds and mattresses destined for the injured at the hospital.

I survived the hell run unscathed, although this was only Day Two of what would become my routine for months to come as I patrolled Soweto in the quest for the real story, rather than the one the *apartheid* authorities were trying to feed to the media.

White faces became an increasing rarity, the only civilians often in convoys huddled behind police anti-riot vehicles that crept cautiously through the sprawling township.

I preferred to travel alone or with a photographer who could grab images while I drove. Occasionally my driving experience proved an asset as we made frantic tyre-squealing getaways.

Often I parked my car at a high vantage point and hunkered down low, peering over the steering wheel and hoping I wouldn't be seen by trigger-happy police or potentially violent mobs. Funnily enough the police scared me more because they were heavily armed, and prone to open fire indiscriminately as they did on this day, bullets whizzing uncomfortably nearby. The children were armed only with sticks and rocks, although they had proved these could be a lethal combination when the flames were fanned by mass hysteria.

The *Rand Daily Mail* developed what was known as the 'riot car', a sinister Chevrolet sedan which had thick Perspex windows designed to deflect rocks and even bullets. Less obvious was a sharp serrated edge underneath it that fortunately was never put to the test while I was driving. If an angry mob tried to overturn the car they'd cut their hands to shreds.

It turned out that the choice of car was unfortunate as it was similar to those used by the police, so people either fled in terror or the car provoked angry attacks. I wanted to talk to locals as a neutral observer and realised I'd never get an honest reaction while driving this car. Besides it was a mobile sauna – the windows didn't open and it had no air-conditioner. Worse still was the fact that I couldn't get decent photographs through the thick Perspex and had to climb out and repeatedly expose myself to danger.

I soon resorted to using my personal car and on one scary occasion, colleague Alan van Rooyen and I were surrounded by a couple of thousand tense and emotional scholars, many armed with bricks.

"Peace my Brothers," Alan kept repeating nervously like a mantra, all his usual wit and sarcasm deserting him.

I could neither drive backwards nor forwards, a wall of humanity crushing up against the car while an argument raged about whether to drag us from the vehicle, or let us go.

"Let's kill them," one aggressive young ringleader suggested, while another youth was a voice of reason: "This is a peaceful demonstration. Tell that to your white brothers and tell them to stop the teargas."

I added my own entreaty: "We're journalists. Our job is to tell your story. "A debate raged, our lives in the balance, until commonsense prevailed and we were waved on, the crowd miraculously opening a path for us.

We let out a collective sigh, our pulse rate gradually returning to normal. That was way too close for comfort but the essential goodness of people had carried the day.

What always scared me was how the mood of a crowd could suddenly swing, as it did before the start of a subsequent commemorative service at the huge Regina Mundi Church in Soweto. I was there to conduct interviews and write a story for the *Rand Daily Mail* when a murmur ran through the crowd.

Somebody had suggested I was a police spy and things quickly turned ugly.

Rough hands grabbed me from behind and I was powerless to escape. Then, as luck would have it, a car pulled up disgorging Desmond Tutu, the diminutive cleric and anti-*apartheid* activist who went on to become the first black Anglican Archbishop of Cape Town, a Nobel Peace Prize laureate and the chairman of the Truth and Reconciliation Committee. With him was prominent local civic leader Nthato Motlana – I'd interviewed both men in recent days and at Tutu's request had attended and photographed his earlier consecration as Bishop of Lesotho.

Like the angel he is, he recognized me and must have said something to soothe my captors: those vice-like hands released their grip and I took advantage of the crowd's indecision to beat a hasty retreat to my car, my heart hammering and legs trembling.

Welcome to Soweto!

CHAPTER FIVE

TERROR AIRLIFT

War is a poor chisel to carve out tomorrow.
— *MARTIN LUTHER KING JR,* CIVIL RIGHTS LEADER

With my heart hammering in my chest, I peered through the foliage, took aim and gently squeezed the trigger, the soldier with his automatic weapon springing into sharp focus.

He was scanning the airfield nervously, his weapon cocked, but fortunately not looking directly behind him. I knew that if he turned around and saw me I'd probably die in a hail of bullets, another news photographer's name added to the list of those gunned down covering wars around the world.

But his attention – and mine – was on the group of black youths marching military-style towards the Air Rhodesia Viscount, its passengers not happy tourists this time but grim-faced guerrillas bound for terrorist training in Tanzania, Cuba or the Soviet Union. Their ultimate goal was to liberate South Africa from oppression by a white minority regime.

I was acutely aware that my huge trigger-focus telephoto lens might look like a bazooka or rocket launcher, prompting an immediate panic reaction. My brain was in overdrive and I suspect I'd stopped breathing … click, click, click and click again. The camera shutter sounded too loud to me but the soldier just metres away remained oblivious to my presence. Click, click, click… Enough! I had the evidence we needed and quietly eased into the waiting car, not risking the noise of slamming the door as investigative reporter Mervyn Rees responded coolly as always and drove off slowly, ensuring we were as inconspicuous as possible.

"I've got the pictures," I announced unnecessarily, feeling elation replacing the fear and adrenaline that had knotted my stomach. Ingrid Norton, the sensuous raven-haired reporter who had first received the tip-off about the airlift of would-be terrorists, turned to smile at me in the backseat. I wound the film out of the camera and replaced it with a fresh one.

The night before, Mervyn, an amateur magician, had been amazing as he performed various sleight of hand tricks. The best was getting locals in the bar to write their names on pieces of paper, which he then set alight and allowed to burn

Photographer Geoff with that trigger focus lens

to ashes before announcing what they'd written. Even to me it was pure magic and they were like children, laughing with delight and never suspecting that in between tricks they were being coaxed into conversation and revealing important information. Where were the South African exiles being hidden, and which airfield were they being flown out of?

"Let's go. I know where it is and what time they'll be leaving," Mervyn announced quietly and we retired to discuss strategy for the next day.

That night I played the prankster and pushed saucy love letters under Mervyn and Ingrid's hotel doors, ostensibly from each other, gleefully waiting to see what their reactions would be.

I sensed a tension at breakfast the next day that hadn't been there before and guessed they hadn't yet confronted each other. Well there was no time for that now; we had work to do.

Our first stop was the Selibe Phikwe town centre and a telephone call to the news editor of the *Rand Daily Mail* in Johannesburg, letting him know we'd hit the jackpot. But the call was premature and I suddenly saw uniforms and guns closing in on us and surreptitiously slipped my film into Ingrid's hand, Inky catching on immediately and secreting it into her bra.

The police were polite during the drive to the local station commander's office and when we eventually sat opposite him, I realized we were up against a cool professional every bit as suave as our Mervyn. Who were we? Why had we been asking questions about South African exiles?

Luckily the *Rand Daily Mail* is respected for its truth-seeking and anti-*apartheid* stance and our interrogator was mercifully unaware of our clandestine trip to the airfield, or we might have been arrested and charged as *apartheid* spies. Instead we were ordered to leave town and gratefully headed south to Gaborone, the dusty capital of Botswana, where we would seek official comment on the presence of South African guerrillas on local soil.

We booked into the Holiday Inn and I requested an interview with Archie Mogwe, the charming foreign minister. Then it was the familiar waiting game known to all investigators and we chose to stay together in one room for security reasons, ensuring nothing could happen to one of us without the others knowing it. All for one and one for all.

The three-day wait was an agony and relieved only by lots of banter and a certain underlying sexual tension. I was attracted to Inky and I imagine Mervyn felt the same, although there was more at stake than romance, and especially for two married guys.

The call when it came was a huge relief. We needed to present both sides of the story although answers to our questions were evasive, which is understandable. Botswana was caught in the middle, while needing to play its part in toppling *apartheid*.

Archie Mogwe was emphatic. There were no military camps and the only people being flown out were women and children refugees. Right! Our film said otherwise but we couldn't breathe a word about the explosive proof we were hiding until we were safely across the border into South Africa.

I felt uncomfortable being devious with a government spokesman I liked and admired, although he wasn't levelling with us either.

How he must have cursed the next day when the *Rand Daily Mail* screamed the headline *Terror Airlift* from its front page, my photograph clearly showing the guerrilla trainees marching to the aircraft – there was not a woman or child in sight!

The story was a sensation, precipitating parliamentary debate and a national strike by Air Rhodesia staff outraged that their aircraft was ferrying 'terrorists', while further repercussions followed in South Africa when ground crews discovered the Viscount was being serviced at Johannesburg Airport.

How could this happen?

We secretly believed that South African and Rhodesian security personnel were entirely happy with the situation and suspected they were monitoring and photographing every passenger boarding that controversial aircraft. We had some good sources – our original 'deep throat' was an air hostess Ingrid Norton knew well.

Running simultaneously with the original *Terror Airlift* story was a penetrating insight into the shadowy world of exiles that fled South Africa under the cover of darkness and entered Botswana illegally without any border formalities.

We interviewed exiles in an anonymous shack near the capital and took no sides, simply reporting what we'd seen and heard, although I subsequently received a warning from Gaborone that a warrant had been issued for my arrest. If I returned to Botswana I'd apparently face treason charges! So I didn't for many years despite my great love of the country as a true African success story and remarkable wildlife paradise.

According to my assessment the most serious blot on Botswana's democratic landscape is the government's inhumane treatment of the San Bushmen in more recent times. It is widely believed that their immoral actions have been motivated primarily by greed for diamonds living beneath the surface of the ancestral lands in the Kalahari Desert that belong to the Bushmen. But that's another story …

CHAPTER SIX

PRAYER FOR RHODESIA

*I'm prepared to die, but there is no cause
for which I'm prepared to kill.*

— *MAHATMA GANDHI,* HUMANITARIAN

Fading tourism posters boasted that 'Rhodesia is Super' although the reality was often somewhat different in the war years leading up to Independence in April 1980, when majority rule swept Robert Mugabe into power as the first president of Zimbabwe.

"It's God's own country," white Rhodesians had often declared with characteristic cheerfulness, perhaps overlooking the fact that their black housekeepers and gardeners were denied voting rights in the land of their birth.

And yet, even at the height of hostilities it was a country characterized mostly by warm and friendly interactions between people of all hues, which seemed remarkable when you consider that the war had claimed several thousand lives from all communities.

For tourists Rhodesia was inexpensive and welcoming, popular attractions including Victoria Falls or Mosi-oa-Tunya, the "Smoke that Thunders"; Wankie Game Reserve where elephants outnumbered people; and Kariba, the vast man-made lake created to generate hydro-electric power and serve as a playground for happy, sun-bronzed holidaymakers.

For many whites the bubble burst the day that the Hunyani, an Air Rhodesia Viscount, was downed with a heat-seeking missile, 38 people dying in the crash with another 10 later murdered on the ground. There were just eight survivors who hid in the bushes, among them 25-year-old Sharon Cole and her five-year-old daughter Tracy.

"I never thought you could see such panic," she confided to me in an interview for the *Sunday Tribune*. "It took four minutes from the time we were hit until the crash but it seemed forever. People said the passengers died on impact: they didn't.

"The nose went into a ditch and broke off; then the tail broke as the aircraft somersaulted; and the centre section rolled over and over. When it had all broken up it seemed to explode. In the mass of flames the screaming went on and on."

Afterwards she, little Tracy and others hid while the terrorists hunted them. "They were laughing and talking and had no qualms about the survivors they had murdered," she recalled, her voice faltering.

Five months later the horrifying nightmare returned with a vengeance when another heat-seeking missile found its target just minutes after take-off from Kariba. All 59 passengers and crew aboard the Umniati, many of them women and children, died when the stricken airliner plunged into a ravine, exploding in a fireball.

In the offices of the *Herald* newspaper in the capital of Salisbury I witnessed distressing scenes of shock and bewilderment.

Through a blur of tears cashier Mrs Pia Potgieter informed a group of men at the head of a queue that there was no space in the newspaper for any more death notices. For years she had dealt with death and condolences, trying to be matter-of-fact, soothing and even cheerful. But this latest atrocity was too much and she broke down and wept. The men were husbands and fathers who had booked wives and children on the aircraft, while they had travelled by road, believing their families would be safer this way.

For Sharon Cole and her hotelier husband Howard it was a final straw. "I flew for the first time a month ago believing it could never happen again. I was horror stricken when it did. I was just beginning to get over it – the nightmares were stopping – then it all came back."

Just hours after the second Viscount disaster I joined journalists and photographers at the Karoi Police Station, where we spotted a white-haired grandmother carrying a machine pistol with the easy familiarity of a handbag.

An escort of three armed personnel carriers had been arranged to take us to the crash site, but one of the vehicles was tossed on its side with the force of a powerful landmine blast. All survived although there were a number of injuries.

Terrorists were somewhere in the vicinity and I was warned not to touch anything: "It could be booby-trapped!"

Leaving the beaten track the Press party was taken on a bucking, lurching ride through spectacularly beautiful country that there was little time to appreciate. Hanging on for dear life we ducked the branches that closed in like menacing fingers. The mood was sombre and brooding.

At one point terrorists' tracks were detected leading to the crash. They were somewhere nearby.

Suddenly the sickening smell of death reached us and we knew we'd arrived. That night, with my immediate story written, I drank to deliberately get drunk for the first and only time in my life, but I couldn't drown the horror or escape that lingering smell of death. It haunted me long afterwards.

The following night I had dinner in an Italian restaurant with a beautiful blonde model and there was a manic quality to our time together, she mourning the loss of her father in a road accident and me coming to terms with what humans are capable of doing to each other.

In the ensuing days I took to finding places for quiet reflection, among them St Mary's Anglican Cathedral in Salisbury.

There I came across a battered black exercise book that chronicled the agony of the country, mirroring the heartache and hope of people of all races. Often the writing was an immature scrawl, punctuated with errors, but always the words were from the heart and could hardly speak more eloquently.

A mother mourned the loss of a son in some bloody, bush skirmish.

A child faced up to the reality that her father was dying from injuries sustained by a landmine explosion.

A lover prayed for a future that wouldn't be alone.

A soldier hoped he would come home again.

The book laid bare the soul, sharing the burden with anyone who cared to stop and read.

The prayer that touched me most deeply was: "Please watch over everyone … I know you took my Luvbug for a reason."

Another alongside the heading 'Air Disaster' said simply: "Goodbye Sue."

Re-reading my *Sunday Tribune* stories I feel an ocean of sadness welling up inside me, although there was also the short-lived joy of Independence just weeks later when jubilant supporters of Robert Mugabe ran through the streets flapping their arms and making crowing noises. The symbol of the political party is a cockerel.

That evening I joined an amazing victory party in Harare Township where we were served crates of beer by a charismatic young black woman, with a ready smile and astonishingly white teeth. She was a seasoned bush fighter who no doubt had her own private horrors although this was a night of pure joy and celebration. The disillusionment and broken promises would come later.

The next morning, with a thumping head, I was among the first in the world to interview Mugabe, filing a story for the *Sunday Tribune* in Durban and another for a respected London newspaper, which went big on it.

Photographs I'd taken of the First Lady of Zimbabwe looking radiant and re-laxed in a floral print dress in the garden of the presidential residence, later appeared on magazine covers around the world.

Back in my hometown, the coastal resort of Durban was experiencing the annual sardine run, which is an amazing natural phenomenon involving the spawning and migration of billions of pilchards in the Indian Ocean along South Africa's

The promise of 1980... with Robert Mugabe the day after
he was swept to power as the new Zimbabwe president

east coast, precipitating a feeding frenzy that attracts bigger fish and a multitude of sharks.

It was a crushing blow to my ego that a small fish consigned my Robert Mugabe scoop to an inconspicuous single column story inside the paper, although maybe that's poetic for a ruthless dictator who has bled his country dry, clinging to power for more than three decades. His sorry legacy is mayhem and murder, land grabs and the economic ruin of a country that really was super and will be again.

CHAPTER SEVEN

SHADOW OF DEATH

Death, in itself, is nothing; but we fear,
To be we know not what, we know not where.

– JOHN DRYDEN, POET

"I'd like to have his problems," I said enviously to my photographer friend Charlie Ward, as we left American Peter Revson to strap himself into the Shadow Formula One racing car at the legendary Kyalami Grand Prix circuit.

I'd chatted briefly to Revson and admired his easy-going charm and free-spirited nature. He had the world at his feet: his gorgeous girlfriend Marjorie Wallace was Miss World; he had Hollywood good looks; was heir to a billion dollar empire and was being tipped as a future world champion.

Minutes later he came storming down the main straight that was famous as the longest and fastest in grand prix racing, the gleaming black projectile squirming under heavy braking, turning right into the sweeping Crowthorne Bend and howling down the hill towards Barbecue Bend.

That was as far as he got. Something went horribly wrong and the car careered into the metal barriers, breaking in two and showering pieces of bodywork as it burst into flames. I was shocked by the sudden violence of it but didn't immediately fear the worst, sprinting towards the crash to capture the first images.

Pausing momentarily I shot the first frame depicting oily black clouds of smoke and billowing flames rising heavenwards. I was puzzled because I couldn't see Revson anywhere.

Running again I reached the wreckage as other race cars stopped, drivers in full-face helmets and flame-resistant overalls and gloves rushing in bravely and attempting to lift a piece of burning car off the barrier. I was standing on a fragment of shattered fibreglass that read *Peter Rev* when the full horror of it hit me. He was still in the inferno. His crumpled body was dragged out and somebody announced hopefully: "He has a pulse." I doubted it and when the ambulance raced away I somehow knew.

A man I'd admired was dead and my images raced around the world, filling the front page of virtually every major morning newspaper. A publishing company in Brazil insisted I give world champion Emerson Fittipaldi every image I had to fly home with to Sao Paulo, an entire magazine produced within days, allegedly to honour a life. It sold magazines and paid me handsomely, although I felt sick in my gut.

I hated the clichéd headlines of the "Shadow of Death" and "Fiery Death at Barbecue Bend." How the hell had they given a corner on a racetrack that stupid name anyway?

A newspaper editor, who was one of the judges for the prestigious Photographer of the Year competition, said I was a certain winner. I'd acted the cool professional and snapped perfect images, automatically compensating for the dark clouds of smoke that could have compromised my exposures. But I couldn't capitalize on his death. It haunted me and I didn't bother entering the competition.

Peter Revson is dragged from the inferno at Kyalami

I also thought long and hard about why a life is suddenly snuffed out and reading a book entitled *The Reincarnation of Peter Proud* somehow resonated with me and seeing the film of the same name reinforced the idea. Living again and again made more sense than my shallow understanding of the religious dogma and propaganda of a typical Christian upbringing.

Life and death went on in the motor racing world and despite Formula One's appalling safety record Welshman Tom Pryce gratefully took Revson's place in the Shadow team.

Three years later, at the same circuit, an inexperienced young marshal carrying a heavy fire extinguisher ran across the main straight to assist with a fire at a point where the oncoming cars were doing 270 km/h. It was suicide and Pryce, a 27-year-old hopeful tucked in behind another car, probably never saw the hand that fate dealt him. The marshal's body was thrown high into the air in a sickening sequence repeated often on the evening TV news. Pryce took the full impact of the fire extinguisher in his face and died instantly.

Sitting at Crowthorne Bend I watched the gruesome scene unfold as a dead driver raced at full throttle towards me before finally colliding with the car of Frenchman Jacques Lafitte as they entered the bend. Lafitte was unhurt but what he saw of his rival in the wreckage was so sickening that he risked death again, sprinting across the track. He kept running, trying in vain to outrun the horrors imprinted in his brain.

Years later my great hero Ayrton Senna, a Brazilian triple world champion, would slam into the barriers while leading the 1994 San Marino Grand Prix in Italy. The suspension rod that penetrated his helmet extinguished an inspirational life and with it my passion for motor sport. He was the seventh GP driver I'd known or interviewed to die on the track.

I'd begun to wonder if death was stalking me, too many stories as a news reporter involving the dead and dying.

When police stormed a Pretoria bank and freed hostages held by a trio of terrorists of the ANC's military wing during the infamous Silverton Siege, I was among the first on the scene. Blood was pooling around the bodies of the dead gunmen spread-eagled on the floor. I photographed a spoon in a cup of still warm coffee, imagining someone calmly stirring their drink before the sudden violence.

Most deaths around me were violent although my father's slow battle with cancer seemed crueller and more painful despite his humour. "If I can't take it with me, I'm not going," he joked.

The last thing I ever saw him do was lift a hand, and just using his fingers, weakly wave to our toddler daughter Bonnie. It would be the last time he saw her and I felt an incredible surge of sadness that he'd never know Tammy who was just a bulge in my wife Carol's tummy.

My Dad was in agony and bleeding from his nose, mouth and ears when I appealed to a nurse: "Please give him some painkillers." It will kill him, she warned, and it did.

My gratitude that his suffering had ended was huge, although I was tormented by the fact that I'd always been too busy to join him and my Mom on weekends away, putting it off despite Dad's entreaties: "Come with us to the Kruger Park. Just for the weekend. It will be fun!"

Days before he'd died he tried to explain what he wanted done to smooth things for his beloved wife Gladys, who he called Glad-eyes. "You'll be fine," I said, taking the coward's way out and refusing to confront reality. How I regretted that.

More than a decade later it was my dear, precious mother's turn and when I received a phone call I was about to strap myself into a racecar on the other side of the country. Instead I engaged in another race and reached her bedside minutes too late, sitting there holding her lifeless hand, uselessly wishing I'd been a more devoted son.

In the last couple of years my wife Carol was a wonderful friend to my mother, although I often avoided visits to the nursing home because I hated seeing the relentless decline into illness and confusion. Another act of cowardice!

Often since I have felt their presence, connecting with my Dad when I've read favourite poetry or heard classical music he loved; meeting 'Mumsy' again whenever under a canopy of stars, remembering how we'd lie on our backs when I was a child and marvel at the heavens. I experienced that familiar loving thrill a couple of nights ago.

With the passing of my parents I could celebrate an end to their suffering and rationalize that it was for the best, also taking comfort in my burgeoning belief in reincarnation. Reading the book *Many Lives, Many Masters* had been a lightbulb moment.

I experimented with a number of guided regressions into previous incarnations and once, when I compared notes with Carol, I discovered that we had both independently experienced the same storyline and characters from a previous life a couple of hundred years earlier. Seems we have known each other forever and it always felt like that, which is perhaps why our many years together were so easygoing and relatively free of conflict.

But despite my convictions about reincarnation, I could still be devastated by death. This was especially true with my great friend Herman Potgieter, a world-renowned aviation photographer who was poised to become my business partner. We'd planned five photographic books together and agreed that I'd manage a successful annual aviation publication he owned.

In 1998 our first aviation project together was to be a photo-feature on the delivery of a pair of Pilatus PC12 aircraft from Switzerland to South Africa. Instead a freak car accident during a televised comparison test between leading four-wheel-drive vehicles overturned my plans. "Sorry Herman, I'll have to stay and sort this mess out," I lamented.

Herman had planned to capture evocative air-to-air images with Mount Kilimanjaro as a backdrop, but apparently bad weather intervened and the two aircraft had to return to Wilson Airport in Nairobi, the pilot of the second aircraft clipping the top of the Ngong Hills immortalised in the movie *Out of Africa*. All nine on board died, three of them people I knew. It was Friday the 13th and the next day was St Valentine's Day when one of the dead, a young reporter taking my place in the aircraft, was looking forward to being engaged.

I'm not superstitious although the accident, coming so soon after the death of another friend and his family in a light aircraft crash, distressed and demotivated me, impacting on my plans for the next couple of years.

Herman's funeral service was a fitting tribute to an incredibly popular personality and involved a flypast of military and civilian aircraft. I doubt if there was a pilot who hadn't known or heard of Herman. Best of all was the reading of a poem written by a young Battle of Britain aviator, John Gillespie Magee Jr, which remains a source of inspiration.

HIGH FLIGHT

Oh! I have slipped the surly bonds of Earth
And danced the skies on laughter-silvered wings;
Sunward I've climbed, and joined the tumbling mirth
Of sun-split clouds – and done a hundred things
You have not dreamed of – wheeled and soared and swung
High in the sunlit silence. Hov'ring there,
I've chased the shouting wind along, and flung
My eager craft through footless halls of air …

Up, up the long delirious burning blue
I've topped the windswept heights with easy grace
Where never lark, or ever eagle flew –
And, while with silent lifting mind I've trod
The high untrespassed sanctity of space,
Put out my hand, and touched the face of God

CHAPTER EIGHT

FERRARI F40 PILGRIMAGE

*I think God is going to come down
and pull civilization over for speeding.*
— *STEVEN WRIGHT,* HUMOURIST AND WRITER

On very rare moments I have experienced that deliciously heightened sense of awareness when my concentration was absolute and I became one with the machine, flying faster and higher than ever before and moving beyond mere mortality.

In a moment like this the exhilaration of speed overcomes the natural fear of dying or getting hurt and everything is instinctive, flowing with a perfection that is pure poetry. It is a Mozart moment that might never again be replicated.

This is not to be confused with pinnacle motoring experiences, of which I've had many, that come simply from driving awesomely fast cars like the Audi S1, which dominated world championship rallying until this breed of supercar was outlawed in the interests of safety. The speed had become so outrageous that too many drivers and navigators were dying.

Looking back on a motoring career spanning decades I still rank my meeting with the Audi rally car back in 1987 as a highlight, the explosive performance shattering all my preconceptions and providing an adrenaline-rush second to none.

On that day I drove the competition car in the company of namesake Geoff Mortimer, who went on to become South Africa's rally champion later that season, thanks to a great talent and his vastly superior weapon.

We tried the Audi at highly illegal velocities along some minor dirt roads through smallholdings near the Kyalami racetrack, between Johannesburg and Pretoria. Geoff showed me the basics and then we swapped seats and I belted and clipped myself into the racing seat and harness.

Revving it up and dropping the clutch achieved instant neck-jolting momentum, launching the car with a ferocity I'd never known before. Although we were on very narrow and slippery sand roads, it hit maximum speed at 8,500 revs per minute in sixth gear in under 13 seconds. We were doing 237 km/h – almost 150 miles an hour – when I tried to shift up.

Geoff laughed: "There are no more gears. That's it!" And yet it had still been accelerating with incredible urgency when the electronic limiter stepped in to prevent the engine self-destructing. It made the most unbelievable sounds, like an enraged parrot in a small cage squawking its fury. I loved it.

Stomping the accelerator I felt all four wheels spin wildly even at 160 km/h. And jumping on the brakes before we ran out of road was equally inspirational. It was like driving into a wall, so powerful were the brakes and so massive the retardation. Wow, this is living, I thought delightedly.

Back home a few hours later, I checked my bank balance, made phone calls and secured a promise from Volkswagen Motorsport that they would build me a rally car in time for the forthcoming 1988 season. I was hooked on the rallying drug, even though I knew my more modest racer would only have a fraction of the speed of the all-conquering Audi.

And yet it wasn't my first season of rallying, or even the Porsche Turbo Cup racers I campaigned at Kyalami that year that were the highpoint, but rather a few hot laps on the other side of the world at Ferrari's famed Fiorano circuit in Italy.

Using all my powers of persuasion, and my position as the founding editor and co-owner of *Drive* magazine, I persuaded Ferrari's PR man to let me loose in the new F40, the fastest road car on the planet and at that stage one of the most exclusive.

A number of wealthy customers had already put money down to buy one and yet none of them had been allowed so much as a test drive. "They're letting you drive it at Fiorano," they demanded incredulously?

I trained for the day like an athlete, exercising, monitoring my diet, going to bed early and cutting out all alcohol.

Finally, when I was collected from my hotel I was nervous but ready, wanting to savour the pinnacle of Ferrari performance around the famous private test track and fervently praying I would not be remembered as the guy who crashed the F40. Others would qualify for that dubious honour later.

Arriving at the Maranello factory I loved the irony of a plaque commemorating the Pope's visit. Only in Italy would a pontiff make a pilgrimage to a car factory, where Ferrari's racing headquarters is a hallowed shrine for petrolheads.

Initially my Italian hosts were tense and almost unfriendly, clearly feeling uncomfortable with the idea of a stranger being let loose in their very fast and expensive piece of machinery. I'd been vouched for by the South African Ferrari agents though, bribing them with the promise of a cover story in *Drive*.

How did I wish to handle the track session? I asked the chief test driver to chauffeur me around the unfamiliar track, showing me the techniques and ideal racing lines through the corners. Then I'd do a few medium-pace laps to learn the

Meeting the Ferrari F40 which was then the fastest street-legal car on the planet

car and circuit. He was fast and flamboyant, and I wondered if I was in the same exalted league.

When I was ready to really go for it he seemed relieved at my suggestion that I do this alone, savouring a great sense of history, knowing that so many legendary world champions had driven the same circuit in red cars adorned with the rampant Ferrari emblem.

The car sounded and felt amazing and I gradually increased my speed until I was powering out of the turns with the back sliding and the engine bellowing as it hurtled the scarlet car from corner to corner.

Everything came together and I established a beautiful rhythm knowing I'd never driven better or faster. Eventually I had the sensation of travelling down a tunnel where nothing else existed but me and this speeding red bullet. It was sublime and almost a God moment.

I'd probably have been intimidated had I realised my every move was being monitored from the pits with advanced electronic timing gear and cameras, seeing if I slid too wide, braked too late or perhaps needed an ambulance despatched to a crash scene.

Waving me into the pits after several hot laps I realized the mood had changed dramatically. First the test driver embraced me enthusiastically and then it was the turn of the deliciously sexy PR lady to dispense hugs and kisses. Had I done as well as I'd hoped, or were they just ecstatic that I hadn't crashed their car? It didn't matter. I was euphoric, knowing I had visited motoring heaven.

We lunched at the famous *Il Cavallino Restaurant* opposite the factory gates where founder Enzo Ferrari had often enjoyed a meal, we three drinking too many glasses of Lambrusco wine amid exuberant conversation. I almost missed my flight, racing flat-out to the airport in a tiny, asthmatic Fiat hire car. After the Ferrari it felt like the engine had been removed although nothing mattered. I was walking on air.

Arriving in London that evening my euphoria remained and was obviously contagious, a gorgeous young woman seeking me out at a party in Kensington. Together we celebrated the simple joy of being alive. Life is good.

CHAPTER NINE

SHIT HAPPENS!

*When we least expect it, Life sets us a challenge to test our
courage and willingness to change; at such a moment,
there is no point in pretending that nothing has happened or
in saying that we are not ready. The challenge will not wait.*

— *PAULO COELHO*, NOVELIST

True to the legend, Camel Trophy 1995 started as a torturefest so punishing that the contestants wondered whether they would survive the first day, never mind a shattering three weeks in a Central American sauna.

Kicking off with 30 hours of gruelling physical challenges near the Lamanai Mayan ruins in northern Belize, competitors from 20 countries ran, climbed, swam and canoed in suffocating humidity combined with searing temperatures of up to 48 degrees Celsius.

A team of three doctors worked non-stop to render medical assistance, setting up drips for contestants who succumbed to heat exhaustion, dehydration and extreme fatigue.

"Make sure you drink a litre of water every hour," they warned repeatedly, one of the medical trio himself collapsing and joining his patients spread-eagled on the jungle floor.

The effects of the heat and punishing physical challenges were devastating. Once I sat down, head slumped, fighting back tears of exhaustion. Perhaps for the first time in my adult life, I wanted to cry, but couldn't possibly show such vulnerability in this testosterone and adrenaline-charged environment.

I too was trying desperately to be the action hero, although like fellow photojournalist Marek Patzer, my main role was actually to generate publicity and supply logistical support to champion skydiver Paul Leslie-Smith and surf shop owner Marc Pincente in the South African 'dream team.'

It was obvious that we had a real chance of grabbing overall victory from the 19 other national teams, all using identical Land-Rover Discovery 4x4s laden with specialist equipment. And I had the advantage of being a highly experienced four-wheel-drive campaigner, with several seasons as a factory-sponsored race driver to my credit.

While it was motoring journalism that had paid the rent for many years, I'd made it my mission to become a fast and skilful 4x4 driver, competing in national championship races and also qualifying as a 4x4 driving instructor. I had plenty of trophies to show that I was made of the right stuff.

Admittedly at 46 I was one of the oldest participants but felt confident that my age was offset by a never-say-die determination forged in the heat of motor sport battle. But this was a different kind of heat. I wondered if Paul, Marc and Marek were surviving any better.

The pre-event literature had tantalised with descriptions of the ancient Mayan civilisation that we would explore along the five-country route through Belize, Mexico, Guatemala, Honduras and El Salvador.

Hidden beneath the towering rainforest canopy, we'd meet the remnants of a remarkable culture that flourished for 3,000 years while Europe languished in the Dark Ages, the Mayans surviving six times as long as the Roman Empire.

Soaring pyramids and massive stone temples and palaces are testimony to amazing artistic and intellectual prowess, along with complex understandings of astronomy and science. But those first days were all about survival for us, rather than an appreciation of history or ancient spirituality.

Nothing had prepared us for this assault on mind and body and even the presence of hairy, hand-sized tarantula spiders and swarms of angry bees and hornets seemed a minor irritation compared to the overpowering heat.

At the end of the 30 hours of special tasks we were placed third and feeling confident, even if Marc and Paul could barely keep their eyes open as the 33-vehicle convoy rolled out of camp, heading for Mexico.

Blinding dust immediately became enemy number two, and the Land Rovers were not equipped with air-conditioners – that would have been too easy – and we had to keep windows open, despite choking dust clouds.

I drove while the others attempted to sleep. Often we moved only a few jolting metres before having to stop and clear fallen trees from the track. The sound of chainsaws was to become as familiar as the cries of the unseen creatures of the night as the convoy avoided roads in favour of obscure tracks that had fallen into utter neglect.

Finally, stopping in the small hours for some freeze-dried food heated on the hot engine we inadvertently pitched our tents in the path of another convoy – this time an army of hungry harvester ants. But we were elated. We were living a dream and Camel Trophy was shaping up to be everything we'd dared hope.

Before dawn we were on the move again, numbed with exhaustion as we crossed into Guatemala. The sadistic pattern was being established. Heat, dust, bone-jarring bumps. Also a sense of wonder at the unstoppable energy of the convoy. The worse conditions were, the more gleeful the organisers.

"We aren't sadists," I was assured, "Camel Trophy is supposed to be tough." To the discomfort of being sweaty and dirty, add blisters, backache and the stings and bites of spiders, ticks, ants and assorted unidentified nasties.

But every few hours there was a fresh experience to send our spirits soaring, like the deafening wake-up call of howler monkeys, which turned out to be quite modest-sized creatures endowed with the booming voices of a King Kong with a megaphone.

And because this fabulous adventure played to our egos, we conveniently overlooked the fact that we were ambassadors for a tobacco brand, sucking up the propaganda and even doing some good deeds.

Guatemalan archaeologist Teresa Chinchilla was one of many who welcomed our presence. "Through you we can send a message to the world to help protect our forest, which is a national heritage, as well as supporting our environmental and archaeological work." And we did, beaming images around the planet of the devastation wreaked by slash and burn agricultural policies that reduced pristine rainforest to farmland that would ultimately supply burgers to predominantly overweight North Americans.

Ever mindful of the need to be more than a stage-managed marketing exercise for a cigarette company, the event funded the building of an environmental research station in El Salvador's Monte Cristo National Park, also providing the manpower to uncover and map an inaccessible ruined Mayan city straddling the Mexico/Guatemala border. So we felt good about ourselves.

Leaving the relative comfort of our 4x4s behind, we hiked through dense jungle, carrying full packs, to the site where we would work continuously in shifts for 48 hours, unlocking secrets hidden for centuries.

The elation of uncovering artefacts, tombs and a temple that dated back to between 300 BC and 900 AD was hugely uplifting; although I was feeling utterly drained and unable to think clearly. What day is it? Who cares?

By now many of us were covered in an ugly heat rash that looked like a severe bout of acne, or were laid low by diarrhoea and vomiting.

Drinking water was being rationed, I had not washed in days, or seen a mirror, and was suddenly aware of an unpleasant sweat smell. Looking around I was startled to discover I was alone.

Not that you are ever alone for long when you are part of an expedition of 134 people. Privacy is a luxury there is little of, even when you hike off with a spade to perform your toilet duties.

I guess it was worst for the three lady competitors and trio of female journalists, thrown in with so many men, but they were a lesson in good humour. I was also to learn lots from outspoken American outdoor adventure consultant Daphne Greene.

"Did you burn your toilet paper?" she once demanded, causing me to cringe with embarrassment. Seeing my confusion and discomfort she went on to recommend that I seek out an important little book entitled *How to Shit in the Woods*.

Soaping yourself in a muddy or polluted river also wasn't on, Daphne rightly arguing about the threat to fish and other life. "The fact that locals do it is no excuse. I know better and have to live with my conscience, however inconvenient," she insisted.

As an editor calling the shots I was used to being centre stage, and here I was in a support role learning about patience, tolerance, sensitivity, sharing and caring.

Learning also never to under-estimate others or the power of the human spirit. At the start we had joked about the flabby, white Swiss TV cameraman and unkindly predicted that he wouldn't last a day. By the end he was a friend we greatly admired.

In fact, we invariably camped alongside the Swiss team and not just because we were all a little in love with geography student Manuela Catalini. When her teammate was sidelined by a deep gash to the leg, and the team journalist ripped ligaments in his leg, it was the now somewhat less-flabby TV cameraman who stepped in to help with tasks that included carrying two full jerry cans of water and a spare wheel over 2 km. To think we'd been so mocking and judgemental.

We also learned never to be over-confident. I guess I'll always remember my embarrassment and the blow to my ample ego when I toppled the Land Rover onto its side while negotiating a deep ditch. We were following a daunting route pioneered by Spanish explorer Cortes nearly 500 years earlier that had never before been driven by four-wheeled vehicles.

If I'd been less impatient and tackled the obstacle on foot first, or had had somebody directing me, I would probably have stayed on four wheels. But I certainly wasn't alone and we lost count of the vehicle mishaps.

"Shit happens," was a common expression, explaining a multitude of injuries to machines, people and egos.

Once my team-mate Marek suggested ditching a spare wheel in favour of a case of beer and I realized he wasn't joking, finally appreciating the magnitude of his craving and addiction, which made his ability to work tirelessly and cheerfully all the more impressive. He cooked for the team and many others while always managing to be the life and soul of the party. He's become a treasured friend, where at

Geoff, Paul, Marc and Marek at the end of the 1995 Camel Trophy in Central America

first I wanted him off the team because he was a heavy smoker. I guess I never saw the irony of being sponsored by Camel.

Along the way we joked that "Winning isn't everything, but second sucks". So you can imagine our astonishment and disappointment when we, the firm favourites, collected three second places for the special tasks, team spirit and overall Camel Trophy award. Team South Africa had been dished up a character-building defeat.

I'd already won my greatest prize though. Lying exhausted on my back one night in Guatemala, I watched a dazzling shower of shooting stars and was suddenly engulfed with a great sense of peace, joy and beauty. I'd had my epiphany and knew that there was much more to life than the trappings of success as a magazine editor, race driver and conspicuous consumer. I realised in that moment that my life had to change: I'd quit my editorship, reassess all my values and commit to making a difference.

I was voted Motoring Journalist of the Year for my Camel Trophy coverage and bought a new Land Rover Discovery although the real prize was my awakening.

Acting on what I knew to be right, and recognizing that feelings are the language of the soul, took longer than it should and I faced an agony of fear and indecision before taking the leap and making far-reaching changes.

CHAPTER TEN

TRUE LUST

Of all the worldly passions, lust is the most intense.
All other worldly passions seem to follow in its train.
— *GAUTAMA BUDDHA,* SPIRITUAL TEACHER

"You even cheat on your mistresses," my secretary Natalie said accusingly, as she juggled my business appointments to accommodate an illicit assignation, reluctantly helping me balance the often conflicting roles of editor, racer, road tester, lover, husband and devoted Dad.

What was I trying to achieve, I wonder? The busyness of my life was insane; pure adrenaline and a reckless spirit of adventure propelling me through each day. Mostly it was fun and my energy seemed boundless, so passionate was I about all my pursuits.

The game had to end though, and it did when a married mistress became pregnant, insisting and hoping I was the father-to-be. Human lives and happiness were at stake and I resolved to change my ways immediately and be a devoted husband once more, cutting off all extra-curricular activities, and especially anything compromising quality time with my children. It was time to take responsibility for my life.

Outwardly a period of normality ensued although increasingly I felt a great emptiness and numbness, mistakenly imagining that I needed a new person in my life to make things right. In a Cape Town hotel room I prayed that I would meet someone to make me feel truly alive again. Careful what you wish for!

Receiving a phone call I headed downstairs to the lobby for a meeting with a friend who was handling the PR for the Daewoo car company of Korea. We were in the Fairest Cape to welcome a supposedly heroic overland expedition from Cairo to Cape Town, although in reality the cars and team had been flown from Egypt to Kenya, cutting out half the mileage and all the serious challenges. It was smoke and mirrors and hugely misleading, the cars proving as disappointing as the misguided marketing campaign.

My world transformed in an instant when a curvy 29-year-old blonde arrived in the foyer, carrying a bouquet of flowers and leaving me dry-mouthed. Is there such a thing as love at first sight? You better believe it. Or was it true lust?

Whatever, I was captivated.

Kate Langdon* turned my world upside down. She was passionate, outrageous and hugely talented, juggling a career making TV commercials with being an occasional mum to three young boys. She was astonishingly generous and could be absurdly irresponsible and destructive. We couldn't get enough of each other.

Just weeks later I approached Carol and said that I wanted out of the marriage; I'd met somebody. "She's young, blonde and has three small children," Carol announced calmly. I was stunned, being certain she couldn't know. "I've been waiting for this," she explained. "A psychic told me a year ago."

Barely months later we were divorced ending almost 20 years of marriage and countless dreams. It was a very painful time. I rode a roller-coaster of conflicting emotions, knowing I'd let Carol and my daughters down badly, but still desperately wanting to be with Kate who also divorced soon afterwards.

I can remember lying next to her while she slept, wanting to breathe the same air she was breathing. I was besotted.

Later my daughters joked about "Dad's Mad Time" and looking back it was the best and worst of times with jealousy, lies, drug-taking and angry fights and accusations, until after three years I knew I had to escape to retain my sanity.

Geoff with great friend Adelle Horler

If anything could have saved the relationship it would have been our weekends of great peace and tranquillity on a small farm she owned in the country. There was no electricity and we harvested herbs and vegetables from the garden, Kate cooking up a storm and creating amazing feasts by lamplight.

When we wanted a bath or an outside shower we heated water with a wood fire and there was a wonderful sense of living simply, sustainably and close to the land. If only we could have kept the city out of our lives it would all have been perfect and we'd have lived happily ever after.

Instead the trauma intensified until I finally moved out and terminated the relationship, feeling massive guilt because her three vulnerable young boys had increasingly come to depend on me.

With the benefit of hindsight I can see now that it was all a gift, endowing me with fresh insights, the relationship intensifying my search for answers and meaning. My spiritual quest shifted up a couple of gears the day Kate walked into my life and I'll always be grateful to her for that. God is found in the most unexpected places…

<hr/>

I resolved to live with integrity and transparency, recognizing the enormity of my deceit during my marriage. Kate's lies were a mirror to my own.

I also returned to nature for healing and when I moved to Cape Town I felt that I had at last come home to myself. Table Mountain was my temple, daily hikes restoring balance and enabling me to go deep within to find my peace.

And then a beautiful person named Adelle Horler, a talented journalist with an unwavering sense of fairness and what is right, came into my life as a romantic partner and fellow adventurer. She remains one of my most cherished friends teaching me much, especially about myself. "Stay real," she often urges.

---

*   Kate is not her real name and I hope that wherever she is, she has healed her hurt and found peace within.

CHAPTER ELEVEN

MEETING AFRICA'S FIRST PEOPLE

The last of the world's First People:
a sad case of neglect.

— *JODY KOLLAPEN,* HUMAN RIGHTS LAWYER

My anguish at what has happened to the San Bushmen is probably only ri-valled by the enormity of my sadness at the disintegration of a remarkable culture and demise of an indigenous people who have much to teach us about communication with the natural world and reverence for even the most hostile of environments.

Their desperate plight is symptomatic of the deep disconnection that afflicts modern humanity. How else can you explain the way we've treated them?

Just a few decades ago it was possible to obtain a legal permit to hunt Bush-men* in the same way that hunters slaughter our wild creatures in the name of sport, so that tells a little of what these marginalized people have been through.

Yes, I appreciate that the only constant is perpetual change and that we live in a world where each species has to evolve to meet new challenges or simply disap-pear from the face of the Earth. But does this mean that the Bushmen too will be extinguished like a candle flame, joining the fast-growing list of extinctions in the 21st century? I harbour this feeling of outraged helplessness and like many other well-intentioned beings feel I should be doing something to counter the evil per-petrated against them.

A precious friend, who claims to see the spirit guides that accompany each per-son on their path through life, insists that one of mine is a Bushman tracker, which somehow resonates with me.

For years I had yearned to spend time with the direct descendants of the leg-endary hunter-gatherers of the Kalahari, who once roamed freely across the larg-est continuous sea of sand on the planet. I'd also devoured the books and read the news items chronicling their downward spiral into widespread substance and physical abuse.

Sadly their story appears to mirror the tragedy of many other First People around the world who have been forcibly separated from their culture and land, among them the Aborigines, the Inuits and Native Americans.

Then, with the flourish of a Government pen in 1999, it appeared that there might at last be an end to the poverty and despair of the Khomani San clan living on the outskirts of the Kgalagadi Transfrontier Park between South Africa and Botswana. On Human Rights Day they won an historic land claim granting them 25,000 hectares of land within the park and 36,000 hectares on outside farms.

Astonishingly, five years later the clan as a group had still never visited their ancestral land within the famed wildlife sanctuary, lacking money to fund the journey and rugged four-wheel-drive transport to negotiate the deep sand. As fortune would have it, Adelle and I were on safari in our 4x4 when we were asked by ecologists Phillipa Holden and Dr David Grossman if we'd help out. Talk about serendipity!

Using a trio of private 4x4s we had space enough between us to transport 19 mainly elderly people to the land they'd known in their youth, while for some young children accompanying them it would be their first glimpse of a traditional way of life they'd never known.

Bouncing along little-used tracks through the red Kalahari dunes I glanced in my rear-view mirror and was greeted by the sight of five wrinkled leathery faces, all wearing happy grins, while a couple of children played out of my sight around their feet. I realized how tiny they are, fitting a backseat that would normally be a tight squeeze for just three adults.

What followed was pure magic, for us at least. We'd planned to withdraw a discreet distance and allow them privacy to reconnect with the spirit of their land and perhaps perform important rituals. But traditional leader Oupa Dawid Kruiper and the elders were having none of that. We were invited to roll out our sleeping bags under the stars in a circle around a raging fire that would hopefully keep us all warm and discourage lions and other predators from venturing too close.

Sleep was impossible, Adelle later noting in a story for the *Cape Argus* newspaper:

> "As jackals howled in the distance the curiously low clicking conversation around the fire continued deep into the night, with many of the group remembering when they were young, roaming freely on this land.
>
> Amid loud laughter and tall firelight stories, there was a joyful sense of a scattered, battered extended family coming together again, in their own place on the planet.
>
> And if the unseasonably warm temperature that night – in a week of below zero pre-dawn cold – was anything to go by, the ancestors were smiling on the gathering of elderly bones."

Dawid Kruiper is the leader of the Khomani San Bushmen

That light shining brightly in the eyes around the campfire reflected a new emotion … hope.

The original claimants had become a marginalized minority group within their own land claim and had already seen others turn a once game-rich farm outside the park into a wasteland after opening it to paying hunters.

"It sounded like a small-scale war down here," said a local farmer.

Oupa Dawid Kruiper has higher aspirations for his clan. "I might be moved away from this land, but I'll never leave it. It's my knowledge, it's in my blood. And it's my pride to give this to our children and our children's children."

Some of the clan's gifts survive and we were taught to use a bow and arrow and shown how to read prints in the sand; Nature's newspaper telling stories of all the unseen comings and goings in the night. The Bushmen are natural story-tellers with a rich oral tradition and there was much fun and laughter as they clowned and mimicked the creatures we were tracking.

These were unforgettable experiences with a people who have so much to share and we hoped we'd be the first of many visitors intrigued by their links with a vanishing culture. Hopefully an appreciation of their skills and heritage would also do much to boost the self-esteem of these downtrodden folks. I for one feel privileged to have shared the wild world of the Kalahari with them and been exposed to their insights.

In the *Cape Argus* story Adelle also quotes anthropologist Paul Myburgh, who spent seven years living with the "tail end of a people' in Botswana's harsh Central Kalahari and became fluent in their language.

He recalls:

"I realized they were seeing 70% to 80% more than I could see. They don't track an animal by following its spoor. They follow the energy lines. They become the animal and feel where it is going. They can track an ant over a rock by following the line of its energy.

"They possess a wonderful, almost inadvertent wisdom and they easily access and live in the realm of the connection between spirit and matter. But then present them with a transistor radio, or an aeroplane spilling passengers from its belly, and these alternatives are so marvellous and incomprehensible that 40,000 years of understanding and knowing is instantly undermined.

"It's as tragic and simple as that."

The result is a people who have lost the depth of their own culture to take on the superficiality of a materialistic new culture. They're twice robbed, Adelle lamented. The younger generation prefers Levi jeans and Coca-Cola to traditional animal skins and precious water extracted from the Nama melon that grows wild and sustains life in the parched Kalahari Desert.

Now there seems to be a glimmer of hope for the surviving traditionalists.

Thanks to the tireless efforts of people like Phillipa Holden and David Grossman funding has been sourced to buy two 4x4 vehicles and launch education and training projects.

Some young women have successfully graduated from a hospitality and catering school while young men have been accredited as tourism guides.

At the beginning of 2012 our makeshift campsite had fulfilled its early promise, a rustic camp at the same spot in the red dunes serving as a sacred meeting place where elders and youngsters can come together to nurture their culture, traditions, language, ancient wisdoms and spirituality. Children are again learning the old stories, songs and dances.

The wheel is turning and Phillipa tells me that real progress is being made in unlocking the potential of this community and their quest for a healthier, happy life that holds promise for future generations. A 'sad tale of neglect' could still be transformed into a success story that South Africa can be proud of. Plans are also well advanced to have their cultural landscape nominated as a World Heritage Site.

"In trying to make things just a little bit right after the grave injustices that have been served on these most gentle and loving of people, the ancestors of all humankind, I hope that we move towards a future that recognizes the sanctity and

The ancestral lands of the Khomani San Bushmen are home to the Kalahari's legendary black-maned lions

connectedness of all life – we cannot harm another without harming ourselves, and in helping another, we then also help ourselves," she said.

---

* Members of the Khomani San clan prefer to be known as Bushmen rather than other seemingly more politically correct descriptions.

CHAPTER TWELVE

ELEPHANT SHOWDOWN

Our inability to think beyond our own species,
or to be able to co-habit with other lifeforms in what
is patently a massive collaborative quest for survival,
is surely a malady that pervades the human soul.

— *LAWRENCE ANTHONY,* AUTHOR OF THE ELEPHANT WHISPERER

"They're coming!" my partner Adelle Horler warned, her tone adding a desperate urgency to her words.

I'd been nonchalantly fiddling with my camera, changing the speed and aperture settings, and looked up to see the start of our worst imaginable nightmare as eight elephants began a deadly charge led by the enraged matriarch.

I instinctively knew that this was not to be a mock charge intended to assert the herd's authority and establish dominance over two puny and ill-advised humans who'd ventured too close on foot. Circumstances couldn't have been more life-threatening, the herd including vulnerable babies and swaggering teenagers intent on flexing their muscles and making an impression.

And unbeknown to us at the time, this family group were already notorious in the area adjoining Zambia's South Luangwa National Park, having twice killed local villagers who'd overstepped some unseen boundary or transgressed some unspoken law of the wilds.

I sprinted, knowing full well that my life depended on absolute speed and a measure of luck, catching up with Adelle and pulling her behind a huge tree where I covered her body with mine, while whispering the emphatic warning: "Don't move!"

"Shouldn't we run", she insisted, breathlessly. "Keep still," I instructed, knowing we could never match the speed of elephants in full charge, the mood of the normally gentle giants transformed into an explosion of aggression as they trumpeted their fury, tusking the ground and raising a dust-storm, heads swaying and ears flapping just metres away from us on the other side of the tree. Also audible were deep stomach rumblings that are part of their system of communications.

In those agonising moments our lives hung in the balance, our ragged breathing and hammering hearts threatening to betray us to the matriarch who would tusk and trample with a power and ferocity no human could possibly survive. Mercifully elephants have notoriously poor eyesight and the position of that large tree couldn't have been more fortuitous, affording just enough cover to keep us from open view.

I've never known such intense or prolonged terror before, the incident seeming to stretch second-by-agonising-second into many minutes although it was nowhere near as long as that. A trio of irate adolescents moved to the right of the tree and we shuffled left, hugging the bark and certain that they'd see us. They were less than 10 metres away and must surely spot us!

All the while a kaleidoscope of options flashed through my brain, starting with the idea of trying to hoist Adelle into the lower branches, but that escape route was discarded almost immediately. Slung with cameras, we'd probably make too much noise and be seen before I could attempt to join Adelle in the lower branches. I was intent on chivalry but also desperately wanted to survive. Besides how high can a full-grown elephant's trunk reach into a tree? I didn't know.

Best be still and keep praying feverishly. I was also trying to communicate telepathically that I meant them no harm and regretted encroaching on their space, promising that if I survived I'd dedicate myself to the well-being of the Earth and all creatures threatened by humanity's arrogance, greed and ill-advised actions.

My only thoughts were of survival and my gross stupidity in putting us in this precarious position. Adelle meanwhile had been imagining tusks rupturing her body; giant feet crushing and breaking bones. "I thought it is going to hurt so much," she admitted afterwards.

Were our prayers answered by some divine intervention; did my attempt at telepathic communication succeed; did the animals take pity on us; or were we just incredibly lucky? Almost as suddenly as it had begun, the storm abated and the elephants settled down and began to wander off and begin feeding again.

Eventually, with our breathing and pulse rate almost under control, we were able to head back towards our vehicle and nearby campsite at Flatdogs, where we recounted our experience to the camp manager.

"Describe the matriarch," he urged, nodding his head knowingly and identifying her as 'Skeeftand,' meaning skew-tusk in a reference to the fact that one tusk pointed down and the other skywards. "She's killed twice before," he confirmed, and since our terrifying ordeal has apparently done so again.

That night we were still badly shaken and constantly replaying our ordeal in our minds as we tried to understand exactly what had happened and why.

"Do you want to sleep in the rooftop tent tonight or on the ground in the dome tent," I inquired, knowing what the answer would be. We'd been alternating

Moments before the charge that could easily have ended fatally

between a ground-based tent and the one on the roof of our 4x4 as part of our hands-on research into the pros and cons of different types of camping, which would be published in *Drive Out*, the 4x4 destinations guide of which we were the founding editors.

After dinner we were relaxing in the rooftop tent, two metres above ground, when we saw the same elephant family headed straight towards us, Skeeftand with her trunk raised questioningly like a periscope as she sniffed the air.

"An elephant never forgets," I quipped, but my humour rang hollow as she moved slowly towards us at eye-level while we peered nervously through a flimsy gauze mosquito-screen window. Surely she must be aware of our nearby presence?

Finally she seemed satisfied, lowering her trunk and continuing to browse nonchalantly on tasty branches until no more than three metres separated us, our eyes wide with concern and pupils dilated in the ghostly moonlight. All eight animals filed past our vehicle and through our kitchen area on those great padded feet that enable them to communicate using infrasound over distances of many kilometres. Despite their towering bulk and the nearness of a camp table and chairs, they picked their way effortlessly through the obstacle course without brushing up against anything. I've always marvelled at how a giant pachyderm can move so quietly and nimbly. They are such beautiful and amazing creatures!

We were quiet for a while, silently counting our blessings and appreciating how good it is to be alive and living in Southern Africa, the cradle of humankind from which modern humans migrated northwards.

I felt incredible gratitude for our near-death experience. Not only was I wonderfully alive, but I had had an important reminder about respecting the rights and personal space of other creatures, and seeing our place in the greater scheme of things with humility.

We are not the centre of the universe but simply a strand in the web of life that is Gaia Earth, our source of sustenance, nurturing and inspiration.

CHAPTER THIRTEEN

SAVING AFRICA'S EDEN

I don't know what your destiny will be, but one thing
I do know; the only ones among you who will be really happy
are those who have sought and found how to serve.

– *ALBERT SCHWEITZER,* HUMANITARIAN AND NOBEL LAUREATE

"You're amazing," my media executive friend declares, shaking his head in wonder. "You have this ability to completely reinvent yourself and you're doing it again."

I smile inwardly, knowing we all have that talent in every moment of each day. And I remember consciously doing exactly that when I volunteered to work free-of-charge for National Geographic's explorer-at-large Dr Michael J Fay, an American ecologist with a very big dream.

My reasoning was simple. I desperately wanted to make a difference and where better to learn than at the feet of a master as I took the first tentative steps from my materialistic world of fast cars to one of treading lightly upon the Earth. The appearance of Mike Fay was a Godsend!

In 1999 he had grabbed world headlines with an astonishing 456-day/3,200 km hike across the heart of Africa during which he braved contact with just about everything that grows, crawls, slithers, swims, stampedes or bites.

He's survived a goring by an elephant, removed countless leeches from his body, met deadly Gaboon vipers and had to swim and wade through crocodile-inhabited swamps, achieving the stature of a David Livingstone and inviting descriptions like the 'Wild Child of Africa' and the 'Vagabond with a Vision.'

Not bad for a refugee from Los Angeles who, as a five-year-old, trekked up rocky inclines in the foothills of the San Gabriel mountains to escape the asphyxiating cloud of smog that blanketed the city.

These hikes were seminal in shaping his later life.

I meet him in 2004 and am immediately captivated. He's charismatic, intense and seemingly oblivious to ego and image. He wears shorts, a T-shirt and sandals, occasionally donning a rumpled lime-green sweater with a very obvious hole in it.

When I've arranged a series of live interviews on breakfast TV, I find him in sub-zero weather in his sleeping bag in the garden; rather than in the comfort of the

Johannesburg mansion that is our temporary campaign headquarters. I shove a mug of coffee into his hands, realize he hasn't time to shave and inform him his first appearance in front of the cameras is in 20 minutes. And we still have to get there.

"Fine, no problem," he assures, slipping into last night's T-shirt and that ventilated sweater.

I'm flustered; quickly discovering that once the cameras are rolling nobody cares about a stubbled chin or hair in need of a comb. Mike is unselfconscious and his passion is infectious. He sees a priceless African Eden that is in urgent need of saving and he knows how.

His epic 15-month trek across Gabon turned out to be a curtain-raiser to the main event of lobbying to save the remarkable wild places he discovered on his walk from Congo across the breadth of Gabon.

Finally, in a New York hotel room, he is face to face with the president of Gabon. "I showed him *National Geographic* photos of his own country and watched his face light up," Mike recalls.

Later, in a dramatic sequel in the presidential palace in Gabon, Mike and his colleagues face a council of government ministers summonsed to an urgent meeting. They're puzzled. What's happening? Is Africa facing a fresh crisis? Who is this soft-spoken American?

Mike shows edited highlights of his great trek that are from another world: towering trees beneath the rainforest canopy, forest elephants, a humpback whale breaching, even hippos surfing the waves of the Atlantic.

It is an insight into an Africa few have seen and he floats the idea of a network of national parks as an extraordinary opportunity to create a sustainable and commercially viable national treasure for future generations.

You guessed it. His vision of 13 national parks is signed into law and later we find him pitching his tent in Washington alongside a busy road into the US capital. A media stunt? No, Mike is escaping the claustrophobic confines of a rented apartment while raising more than $100-million to fund the new parks. Wow!

Now with the logistical backing of The Bateleurs, a non-profit organisation of volunteer pilots flying mercy missions for the environment, he is applying the lessons learned in Gabon to all of Africa.

Africa MegaFlyover, which I'm helping launch and co-ordinating the publicity for, is nothing less than an audacious plan to fly a little Cessna aircraft in a series of transects over a multitude of landscapes that are among the most beautiful and richest on the planet. The massive undertaking, which involves capturing digital images every few seconds, is sponsored by *National Geographic* and the Wildlife Conservation Society of New York.

I work crazy hours, generate huge publicity and Mike and Austrian co-pilot Peter Ragg fly the equivalent of three times around the world, creating an aerial portrait of humanity's footprint. Later, scientists working with Mike, study 108,641 images and formulate plans to spark conservation action wherever necessary in areas that are either untouched or in danger of being lost to our children's children.

I'm surprised and deeply moved when Nora Kreher, the visionary founder of the volunteer environmental air force, calls me to the stage during the media launch of MegaFlyover, announces to all: "Geoff is now an honorary member of The Bateleurs."

The inspiration for this conservation air force is one of Africa's most magnificent eagles, and the idea is that nothing escapes the attention of these aristocratic birds. I'm apparently one of only two Bateleurs who isn't a pilot or an eagle.

Some weeks later Nora tries to persuade me to take over the running of the organisation as chief executive, which I decline, knowing she was born to fulfil that role for as long as she's able.

Instead I focus more and more on writing about the environment, until one day I decide I've had it as a motoring journalist and dump all my files, including thousands of photographs of cars and motorsport. Motoring has been my passion for decades and still pays my bills. Have I made a terrible mistake?

My cellphone rings the next morning and it is PR man Roger Houghton. "Geoff, Toyota is planning to launch off an environmental platform with the introduction of the Prius hybrid car and we don't have anybody on our staff as passionate about it as you. Would you be prepared to help as a consultant?"

I'm stunned. Does the Universe work this fast? I wonder for a moment if I'll be a front man for a greenwashing exercise and decide we are both taking important steps in a new direction, Toyota South Africa and I.

I write the chief executive's speech and the media releases for the Prius, as well as demonstrating the innovative car to movers and shakers in the environmental world.

When I meet with government officials from Environmental Affairs, I ask why more isn't being done to clean the beaches. "We lack the resources," I'm told and I establish exactly what is needed.

Another phone call and Roger Houghton confirms that Toyota will supply vehicles and fund the printing of information brochures. On a picture-perfect day I drive a Toyota pick-up truck around Robben Island, the renowned world heritage site that imprisoned Nelson Mandela for many years. I'm loading bags of litter collected from the island's beaches by an army of schoolchildren, knowing that similar cleanups are happening simultaneously right around South Africa's beautiful coastline.

It feels good and I give thanks to be part of a global initiative of caring Earth citizens.

CHAPTER FOURTEEN

KILIMANJARO

*When we reach the mountain summits, we leave behind us all
the things that weigh heavily on our body and our spirit.
We leave behind all sense of weakness and depression;
we feel a new freedom, a great exhilaration,
an exaltation of the body no less than of the spirit.*

—*JAN CHRISTIAAN SMUTS*, STATESMAN

Big, icy snowflakes are tumbling from the heavens and I feel choked with emotion as I straddle two amazing worlds – I'm snug in front of my laptop writing this at my temporary winter home in Findhorn, northern Scotland, although my heart and soul are halfway around the planet on Uhuru Peak, the summit of Mount Kilimanjaro.

Uhuru is the Swahili word for 'freedom' and is the tantalising promise to all who climb Kilimanjaro and breathe the rarefied air on Africa's highest peak. The word is melodic and rich in symbolism, being synonymous for me with Life's great challenges and rewards, while the mountain itself has all the credentials to stir the heart of any adventurer, philosopher or poet.

At 5,895 metres Kilimanjaro is the world's tallest free-standing mountain and one of the largest and most dramatic volcanoes to emerge from the Earth's crust, the central cone soaring more than five times the height of Table Mountain. And nowhere else on Earth will you experience the mystique of a snow-capped mountain at the equator, thrusting through the clouds above vast sun-baked grassland plains that are home to the famed Serengeti wildebeest migration which has been described as The Greatest Show on Earth.

The idea gradually took hold until it was an all-consuming passion that wouldn't leave me alone. I had to climb Kilimanjaro and honour a lifelong dream ignited by a boyhood meeting with Sir Edmund Hillary, who with Tenzing Norgay Sherpa became the first to stand on the summit of Everest and the world.

His advice to others was: *"Go and find your own Everest… it's not the mountain we conquer but ourselves… you don't have to be a fantastic hero to do certain things. You can be just an ordinary chap, sufficiently motivated."*

That resonated. I was 55 years old and definitely no athlete or mountaineer. I had spent too much of my life at the wheel of fast cars or rugged four-wheel-drives, only discovering the joy of hiking and high places after I'd made a life-changing move to Cape Town five years earlier. I'd even joked: "Why would God give me Ferraris, Porsches and 4x4s to play with, if she expected me to walk?"

Yeah, it was a great leap into the unknown and probably well overdue for a middle-aged motorist mired in his comforts. It was time to push the envelope and see what I was capable of – to test my courage, determination and newfound fitness.

I needed to learn more about myself and see whether I was made of The Right Stuff. And maybe Kilimanjaro would be a stepping stone to bigger things. In stark contrast with most other legendary high mountains, Kili is unusually accessible, welcoming hikers of all ages from all walks of life, while the six main routes require neither technical climbing experience nor ropes and special equipment. Only the notorious Arrow Glacier section, which was closed some years back for safety reasons and is now very tightly controlled, calls for mountaineering skills.

I suspect that ego plays a big part in my choice of Machame, the longest route at 90 km and I can honestly say I was never tempted by the popular Marangu or 'Coca-Cola Route', which is unique in featuring basic overnight huts instead of tents carried by your porters. Nobody has ever accused me of taking the easy option.

Choosing a tour operator was also easy as I'd become friends with John Addison of Wild Frontiers and seen his commitment to uplifting local communities that depend on guiding and portering jobs for their economic survival.

Was I ready? As with many of my planned contests, ranging from competing in the international Camel Trophy 4x4 torturefest to representing my country in the Malaysian Rainforest Challenge, my starting point was a week of detoxing and strategising at the St Francis Health Centre near the beautiful coastal resort of Port Alfred.

I'm a great believer in the process of cleansing the body of toxins and flushing out the old in preparation for new ideas and challenges, also greatly appreciating the wisdom and guidance of Anneliese Cowley, the Austrian-born founder of St Francis. She radiates love, compassion and a healing energy, also having developed an intuitive ability to home in unerringly on any illnesses or blockages.

She's a great gift and we share the understanding that health isn't just an absence of disease, rather an enthusiastic embracing of life.

I left her feeling energised and ready for the mountain, following up with a visit to the Sports Science Institute and tests by Wayne Derman, the doctor to the South African Olympic squad. He confirmed acceptable levels of fitness and warned of the potentially lethal effects of altitude and Acute Mountain Sickness (AMS), which affect different people differently, and some hardly at all.

Should I take a medication which reduces the chances of suffering altitude sickness and reduces its severity? "It's a personal choice," Wayne suggested.

My booking provided a night's hotel accommodation on either side of the six-day mountain adventure and I noticed the guests were divided into two main camps – those who were quietly and nervously preparing for the next day and those who'd faced their demons and tested themselves, the latter group invariably being loud and boisterous and with good cause. It was the toughest and most amazing thing most had ever done.

Our adventure starts in shorts and T-shirts in the same hot, muggy conditions you'd expect on a wildlife safari into the nearby Serengeti National Park. Then it's an ever-changing spectacle as we trek higher and higher through lush and often rain-drenched forest, into misty and foggy heather, moorland, alpine desert and finally the arctic summit conditions of freezing nights and burning sunny days.

Initially I feel unstoppable and the guides and porters gently caution me to slow my pace. "Pole-pole," pronounced polay-polay, is Swahili for slowly and it becomes a mantra.

The first day is a stunning 19 km hike beneath the forest canopy and I finally emerge into the open to find our team of porters pitching tents and preparing supper. These are the real unsung heroes of the mountain who trek up again and again carrying huge loads and often wearing inadequate protective clothing.

We're in great spirits although I have a moment of extreme irritation when I stand in some human excrement. Be warned that the toilets are the least attractive aspect of a summit bid with often inadequate facilities and too many upset tummies. They're rudimentary wooden structures with a square hole in the floor that you squat over. I'm squeamish at the best of times and in one loo the faeces is heaped higher than floor level. Ugh!

With the benefit of hindsight I'll insist on taking a portable loo and screen in future and provide employment for another porter.

As it is we are 11 in all and supported by a team of 32 guides and porters.

Incredible friendships are being forged and valuable life lessons learned.

By the end of Day Two, which is only 9 km long, the six-and-a-half hour climb to 3,840 metres brings the first signs of altitude sickness with some of us complaining of queasiness and headaches. I feel great.

Day Three is the 40th birthday of a caterer from Amsterdam who is deeply moved by the gift of friendship from virtual strangers. The support team sing to him in Swahili and I make him a present of two pairs of warm thermal socks.

But Day Four is when we see what we are really up against. The higher reaches of the mountain have been shrouded in cloud and mist and I wake before dawn to

The sign that says it all... Congratulations. You are now at Uhuru Peak, Tanzania. 5895 metres

the spectacle of Kilimanjaro totally exposed, my gut churning at the awesome bigness of the mountain. I'm scared and have moments of uncertainty. I'm the oldest in our group by far. Am I up to this?

So, it's sort of like life. You're sometimes frightened, often exhilarated and give it your best shot.

Day Four is the best. The sun is shining and its 15 km and nine hours of walking, starting with a two-hour scramble upwards against a backdrop of waterfalls. The sun glints off the snow and glaciers above, beckoning.

Much to my astonishment there's cellphone signal and mine beeps. The SMS message fills me with joy and fresh resolve: "Dad we love you and are proud of you."

By now we're desperately cold and tired, falling into our tents at 8.30pm on a bleak rocky ledge, the howling wind flapping the fabric noisily. Sleep eludes me and three hours later we're roused with hot soup and a snack. It's time; all of us feeling butterflies in our stomachs.

Our summit bid begins at midnight. The wind is even more ferocious, although the icecap glows in the moonlight and the stars are impossibly close and bright. I see a trail of little fireflies and realise they are the headtorches of trekkers who've started ahead of us. Was there ever a more beautiful night?

We trudge wearily upwards at snail's pace in what's known as the Kili shuffle. Breathe in, breathe out; breathe in, breathe out; then take a couple of steps and start again.

Once when we stop for a rest I decide to stretch out and I immediately feel a hand shaking me urgently. "Don't go to sleep," the fear being that I might not wake again.

We're all too tired for decency and decorum. If you need to pee you do it practically on the path in sight of the others. But we won't have to worry too much about peeing as our water intake has been cut off, our water bottles freezing solid!

Dawn is breathtaking and we gaze in wonder at where we've come from and how far. Now it's little more than a kilometre to Uhuru Peak.

I've never felt so tired, so utterly drained. We trudge on and suddenly we're there. The feeling of achievement and gratitude is overwhelming, the beauty astonishing. I fight back tears, overcome with pride for my fellow adventurers who have endured so much.

One woman makes a call to a school thousands of kilometres away and weeps unashamedly when she tells her two young children: "I've made it. I'm here on the top of Africa … Yes, it is so beautiful."

CHAPTER FIFTEEN

MANDELA MAGIC

I dream of an Africa which is in peace with itself.
— *NELSON MANDELA,* FORMER SOUTH AFRICAN PRESIDENT

"The President wants to meet the team ... now!" The telephone call precipitates mild panic as the four of us are scattered around Cape Town running last-minute errands; the start of the high-profile *African Connection Rally* just hours away.

Radio and TV personality Bob Mabena and I are ready and it is agreed we'll race ahead to the nearby Groote Schuur Estate that houses the President and leading lights in his Cabinet. Jay Naidoo, South African Minister of Broadcasting and London-based telecommunications executive Navin Kapila will follow within minutes along with any of our media entourage we can find.

Getting through security is easier than anticipated, the mostly white former *apartheid* men expecting our arrival and directing us into the beautiful Cape Dutch gabled building that is part official Presidential residence, part museum.

Bob and I get along famously from the start, although it is obvious we are just making nervous small talk while awaiting our amazing President and world icon.

When Nelson Mandela appears he is unheralded and unescorted and he is wearing his characteristic wide grin and bright African print shirt. Beaming hugely, he extends his hand in greeting. "Welcome, welcome," filling the large room with his even larger presence.

I think of him as Madiba, his clan name, and somehow *Mister President* seems too formal for a man noted for his warmth and friendliness to all he meets. I'm not sure how to address him.

He asks me questions and for the first time ever I'm completely tongue-tied, stumbling over my words and gratefully allowing Bob to come to the rescue with his easy-going charisma.

Knowing that Bob has heartthrob status within the black community he stresses the importance of reaching out and inspiring young people.

Clearly he's delighted with the scale of our undertaking to drive two Mitsubishi 4x4s from the northern tip of Africa to its southern extremity, while putting positive images of Africa on TV screens around the world.

Nelson Mandela welcoming Geoff at the Presidential residence in Cape Town during 1999

"Have you made any special arrangements in Libya?" he asks, immediately promising to make a call to his controversial counterpart Muammar Gaddafi.

When Jay appears it's obvious they are good friends as well as political allies, Madiba delighting in sharing time with the former trade unionist and political firebrand.

We help the President into one of the team's promotional shirts and his charming wife Graca fusses over him, adjusting the collar so he'll look right for the inevitable photo call.

A month later we've achieved what some believed impossible when we respond to another Presidential summons, basking in enthusiastic congratulations and again posing at the top of the stairs with the most revered personality on the planet.

There's much to tell and Jay has been right: "We are going to have the experience of a lifetime," he promises at our first meeting, an impossibly short three weeks before a televised trans-Africa expedition that boasted neither vehicles nor a route at that stage. But a generous budget and the force of his optimism, along with the efforts of an army of behind-the-scenes lobbyists and supporters carry the day.

Whooping with joy and hugging his tearful wife, an emotional Jay drives us off the starting ramp at Bizerte in northern Tunisia. "We've got to succeed," he vows, knowing that we will despite doomsday prophecies about the wars in Sudan and Ethiopia, terrorism in Egypt, bandits along the way and the notorious 'long rains' that could strand us in a quagmire in northern Kenya.

The characteristic grin is never far away, although there are moments of intense seriousness, sadness and even loneliness.

I sometimes feel I'm intruding when he speaks on the satellite phone to Kami, 6, Shanti, 4, and his lovely French-Canadian wife Lucie, but how could it be otherwise when we are together for long, long hours every day?

Life in a strange country, married to a politician who is rarely around, hasn't always been kind to Lucie and the family has had to cope with her emotional collapse.

Jay is also grappling with the idea of quitting mainstream politics. "What do you think I should do, Geoff," he asks more than once. "You're the chief, I'm just one of the Indians," I joke in a reference to the fact that I'm the only paleface among the four of us.

Often the conversation in the car is light-hearted, silly even, and Jay loves chatting on the car's radio, poking fun at 'Lord Geoffrey' and his attention to detail, or laughing uproariously at Bob's superb impersonations of Mandela and other politicians.

But there are many serious moments for Jay. "I don't want to wake up one day and say what did I achieve with my life? It is important to ask that question quite early."

"I've been trying to work out my future. The reality is that my wife had a nervous breakdown and suffered from depression ... I missed the first words that Shanti spoke, the first steps she took, and there was a time that I couldn't communicate with my own kids who were speaking French to their mother. If you can't communicate with your own children you're not going to be very productive with anything else you do.

"The most important thing is to be happy with yourself and to be of service," he says. "I grew up with a notion of serving in society. That's something that my mother rubbed off on me. She was a very humble woman but one who taught me the greatest lessons, especially about humility, honesty and integrity.

"I'm driven by change and change that embraces people," he confides. "Some of the most important lessons I've learned were from people who had very little education, including rural hostel workers who were largely illiterate. It is amazing what they became, the skills they acquired, and their hunger for knowledge when given the opportunity.

"The greatest thing for me to see was workers who were once powerless arguing a very sophisticated position in a collective bargaining situation."

With Jay somewhere in the Sudan

The youngest of seven children, he learns much from his older brothers and sisters and their friends, with the family's eviction from the Durban suburb of Greenwood Park under *apartheid's* Group Areas Act being a painful reminder of the times. Jay is just four years old.

Ironically, although my white world is far removed from Jay's, I live in the same area and remember my outrage as a five-year-old when classmates at Greenwood Park Primary taunt me with the suggestion that my best friend is 'Coloured,' a reality my parents confirm that night.

Jay recalls: "It hit me later when I couldn't go to that theatre or get on that bus, but my mother treated everyone equally. I was taught that if something is wrong you should stand up and speak out; and that's what politics should be about – integrity. Friendships must also be built on morality and honesty.

"Now that we have achieved our freedom in South Africa, we have to develop a respect for our environment and work out how to use it in a sustainable way. There is such profound beauty in our country."

Jay and I plan a lengthy camping expedition but in the end compress it into a weekend, meeting up with my environmentalist friend Clive Walker in the Waterberg wilderness area. Jay is deeply moved by the experience and laments: "What we have achieved in the modern world is tremendous advances in technology and yet people are searching desperately for something that is missing in their lives and that is spirituality."

Again his mother's teachings come back: "Every religion has the same basic foundation. All are tributaries of the river of humanity that takes us to this ocean of goodwill. We must look at our fellow man as being of the same fabric and consider: How can I help that person."

I marvel that Jay is the real thing – a committed idealist and an unexpected friend. It's no surprise that Mandela recognised the part he could play in setting South Africa free.*

---

* Jay Naidoo quit politics and is chairperson for the Global Alliance for Improved Nutrition (GAIN) because he believes "the core of determining our global development health is malnutrition and hunger which affects two billion people in the world. It's about human dignity, human rights and social justice whether a parent has the ability to put food on the table for our children each day."

CHAPTER SIXTEEN

TIMBUKTU TO TABLE MOUNTAIN

I learned that courage was not the absence of fear,
but the triumph over it.
The brave man is not he who does not feel afraid,
but he who conquers that fear.

— *NELSON MANDELA,* FORMER SOUTH AFRICAN PRESIDENT

"Go to Timbuktu? I'd rather poke my eye out with a dead fish," the editor of *Fairlady*, a prominent lifestyle magazine declared when Adelle announced her intention to travel down the wild west of Africa, from Dakar to Timbuktu to Table Mountain.

Earlier I'd met with similar enthusiasm while trying to sell the concept: "You want sponsorship for a journey to a mythical place that doesn't actually exist?"

Timbuktu, or Tombouctou as the French prefer, does sometimes get a seriously bad rap, Bob Geldof of Live Aid concert fame asking at the end of a tour of the fabled Malian city: "Is that it?"

OK, it isn't Cape Town, I'll agree, but this dot on the West African map, where the life-sustaining River Niger meets the shifting sands of the Sahara, does have compelling credentials. It was once regarded as the remotest outpost on the planet, boasting fabulous wealth and streets paved with gold: claims that couldn't be disproved because nobody could find the place, or else died at the hands of fearsome Tuareg tribesmen before they could tell the tale.

Of course, I'd intended to change all that, not only finding Timbuktu, but navigating my way home safely to the continent's south-western tip in an epic expedition that would test my own courage and resourcefulness, while sending out positive messages from a continent that often grabs headlines for all the wrong reasons.

Africa isn't only about war and famine, also being home to wonderful people who can teach us so much about living simply and joyfully. I hoped my adventure would demonstrate that and simultaneously reinforce my growing reputation as an overland expedition guide.

Nissan, a potential sponsor, loved the idea but insisted that I tow caravans behind a convoy of their vehicles and complete the massive undertaking in an

76

improbable three weeks on a budget better suited to a weekend outing. End of discussions.

Toyota adopted a more realistic approach once I'd convinced their big-thinking PR man that the place existed. "Let's do it," Roger Houghton urged, immediately visualising his vehicles against exotic African backdrops like the Grand Mosque in Djenne, the largest and most iconic mud building you'll find anywhere.

He came to the party with money, vehicles and characteristic enthusiasm, the sponsorship including two rugged Land Cruiser pickups and a pair of proudly South African Fortuners built at the company's factory in Durban. 'If anybody can make this work, you can," Roger said in a monumental vote of confidence.

When 4x4 MegaWorld stepped in with the generous supply of outdoor equipment, including pop-up rooftop tents, we were in business.

To assemble my dream team I started with my great travel companion Adelle, a journalist and ex-partner who'd be responsible for publicity; resourceful inventor friend Colin Brown (mechanic); ex-military man Johan 'Goose' Goosen (security); paramedic Hugh Price-Hughes and general practitioner Pankil Patel (medical).

Early in the planning we realised that if we didn't have a TV crew along, it would be like winking in the dark. We'd know what we were doing, although nobody else would. And this is where Life became more interesting and the undertaking vastly more expensive. In a bit of inverted racism so typical of post-*apartheid* South Africa, the national broadcaster insisted that the TV series be presented by a black face, despite a queue of accomplished palefaces eager for the job.

Initially there were no takers. The idea of roughing it for at least two months through some countries more famous for violence and political instability wasn't universally popular, although in the end charismatic *Idols* presenter Sami Sabiti stepped forward, accompanied by his lovely wife Melony and energetic TV cameraman Tim Chevalier. I'd never heard of Sami but my daughters assured me: "He's hot and will be great."

The ultimate spin-off was a successful TV series *Go South: Timbuktu to Table Mountain* which only hinted at the off-camera dramas during the amazing 16,000 km, 12-country, 62-day adventure. It was so popular it's flighted at least three times I know of!

I was really excited about Sami coming on board although within a couple of days it was apparent that all was not well in Paradise. We didn't get on, partly because I didn't share Sami's conviction that he was a celebrity superstar who belonged in five-star hotels rather than a rooftop tent, and didn't need to help with menial routine duties like washing up after meals. I'd made it plain from the start that we all needed to muck in.

The tension between us was palpable and it frustrated and upset me that Sami wasn't embracing what I saw as an opportunity of a lifetime for all of us. I didn't want one person's negativity to compromise a vast undertaking involving many others, including diplomats and Toyota dealerships along our route. This was no longer just a personal dream but a major marketing and goodwill initiative.

I mustn't fail, that gnawing fear being far greater than worries about physical dangers.

Just weeks earlier, I'd provided four-wheel-drive backup for a high-profile promotional adventure in which a trio of Mini cars were driven from Johannesburg to their birthplace in Britain. The expedition leader was a friend who showed a side of his personality I hadn't seen before; frequently losing his temper, yelling at team members, threatening them with physical violence and once deliberately accelerating through a heavily armed roadblock in Egypt. That could have got us killed!

I vowed that I'll learn from his mistakes and ensure my expedition flowed smoothly with the minimum of conflict, despite the fact that eight of us would be living in close confines, at times under conditions of extreme stress.

Mercifully what *Go South* audiences enjoyed was an insider's view of a remarkable African odyssey, artfully introduced by a charming and professional presenter. Sami is good at what he does and I guess he was only being human when he was scared, craving a hot shower or dealing with his ego.

With the benefit of hindsight I can see that he was holding up a mirror to my own issues of ego and needing to be in control. Perhaps also voicing fears I never openly expressed.

Hopefully we all look back on that gruelling drive fondly; also remembering important elements censored from the TV series. Sami skilfully directed and presented eight episodes although in the end the broadcaster screened only seven. Instead it presented a dishonest and one-sided picture, cutting out graphic footage of the rape of the rainforests by the logging industry; cruel insights into the bushmeat industry which includes the sale of endangered primates; and the presence of guns everywhere, some of them protecting us from armed bandits.

Admittedly I secretly worried that I might be exposing us to extreme danger, especially in the war-torn Democratic Republic of Congo (DRC) where more than a million have died in recent years. But I had faith we'd be protected and confidence that nothing important had been overlooked in more than a year of meticulous planning.

"Africa, she is broken," somebody quipped, but the truth was that our remarkable journey served to intensify my hope and optimism, rather than heightening any fears that we might come to a sticky end. Or that we might fail, our vehicles mired in the mud, broken down or hijacked by bandits.

Instead kindness and good-natured curiosity were encountered almost everywhere, and humour found in the most unlikely situations – even when our Malian guide Mohammed Number 5 (it's a popular name) finally admitted we were lost. "There's only one road to Timbuktu," he insisted, later conceding that he's never travelled there by road.

Just then a robed and turbaned man and woman on a camel emerged from the dunes, seeming astonished by our presence. Tombouctou? He pointed in the exact direction indicated by our Garmin GPS, a faint and meandering camel path eventually leading us through the dunes to the mystical city where the governor of Timbuktu and local dignitaries welcomed us with a dinner under the stars, spread out on carpets on the sand. It was magical, even to a vegetarian hiding his horror at confronting four sheep carcasses!

What followed is a kaleidoscope of amazing adventures in which we adopted a scrawny puppy who was smuggled through countless borders in a rucksack, the lovely Princess Niger becoming an important unifying force in a team that was anything but united. Who could fail to respond to the love and tail-wagging eagerness of a puppy?

Every day was memorable. We survived an electrical fire aboard one of the 4x4s; braved searing 50 degree Celsius heat in the Sahel; hunkered down during fearsome sandstorms; met forest elephant and orphaned gorillas in Gabon; and were escorted through bandit country in Cameroon by heavily-armed soldiers in

Soldiers travelled on the rooftop tents of the Toyotas through bandit country in Cameroon

The Timbuktu expedition team celebrate their Equator crossing in Gabon with a joyful jump

bullet-proof vests and tin hats. The barrel of an automatic weapon pointed out of the front passenger window of each vehicle, while soldiers lay spread-eagled on the rooftop tents with their weapons aimed menacingly ahead.

When we didn't have soldiers or police escorting us through known trouble spots, I ran ahead with an understanding that if the lead vehicle was ambushed, we'd give a Mayday signal over the radio. The idea then was that the convoy would stop so Goose could take over and wait for a further signal from us, or retrace the route to find help. Luckily it never came to that and I never compromised Adelle's safety, although she was up for anything and everything. No wonder I love her to bits.

Because of the risk of landmines in Angola we often had to stay on the road, not even risking pee-stops in the bushes alongside, although there was abundant compensation in spectacular landscapes, fabulous impromptu beach campsites and some of our best campfires under the stars.

I guess each of us has personal highlights, although we all rated Mali, Gabon, Cameroon and Angola among our favourite countries.

Unforgettable memories included our first sighting of the Grand Mosque in Djenne, the imposing mud building being closed to infidels like us. I arranged for someone to sneak us in via a discreet back entrance, realizing our deception has been discovered when our shoes, which had been left at the door, were confiscated. Oops! Only after profuse apologies for our transgression were we able to reclaim our footwear.

Often we camped; sometimes in the dunes or alongside mighty baobab trees, and invariably locals found us. If we'd landed in a spaceship we'd have created no greater impact than with our four vehicles so conspicuously attired in equipment and sponsors' decals.

Villagers invariably sat in a polite circle watching us like the visiting circus we were. If you needed to go for a pee, you'd be followed, so we tried to strike the balance between friendliness and maintaining some privacy.

In one remote village in Cameroon we drove into a crowd of angry men and a line of trucks queued up at a peage, or toll. As we fingered our money, ready to pay, there was an outraged chorus in French and many wagging fingers. The truckers were blocking the way and quite rightly refusing to pay a toll fee to traverse a dirt road in a poor state of repair. They demanded that we join the boycott, convinced we could spotlight their plight with our cameras and satellite telephones.

It was getting late and we couldn't afford to be stranded for days, so a plan was hatched. Two local villagers climbed in with us and we backtracked and eventually bypassed the toll altogether, crashing through the bush and back onto the road some distance ahead. We sped off to loud cheers from the striking truckers.

That night we camped in pouring rain on a soccer field in a tiny village, with the kind permission of the chief. The poorest people are often the most generous, giving freely of whatever they have.

Always we reciprocated, digging into our ample larder and medical supplies.

I loved the wild unpredictability of it all, whether it was crossing rickety wooden bridges across raging rivers or smuggling our puppy through borders in a rucksack slung nonchalantly over someone's shoulder, while others created a distraction for the guards and customs officials.

It was the time of the Football World Cup so we all shared a common language with animated talk of last night's game thawing even the chilliest of receptions at borders or roadblocks. If talk of soccer didn't work, mention of Nelson Mandela invariably broke the ice. Is anyone more revered?

We are all brothers and sisters and we are all Africans, despite our differences. I felt that strongly and hoped the message would reach television audiences.

More than once I was called upon to make a speech and when a reception was held in our honour at the High Commission in Cameroon, I addressed a visiting South African parliamentary delegation, their leader moved almost to tears. She praised our courage in building bridges in Africa and it all felt so worthwhile.

The Toyota Convoy at the Grand Mosque in Mali which is Africa's largest and most iconic mud building

There were many moments of anguish, though, especially when confronting the reality of the bushmeat industry. Once we bought a young antelope for $20 and then set it free a few kilometres away, inevitably sparking debate about whether we were simply encouraging the bloody bushmeat business. After feeling the frightened animal's heart hammering in its chest it seemed right to save that one life.

Unexpectedly I was as upset by the destruction being wreaked on the rainforests, which are the lungs of our planet. The sight of so many ancient trees being felled is every bit as disturbing as the plight of the animals. How can we be so cruel and short-sighted?

Once, maybe in reaction to all the violence visited upon the natural world, I announced over the car's radio that we were stopping to hug a giant baobab. Sami thought this silly, but I appealed for everyone to humour me and see if our 16 linked arms could reach around the vast girth of the tree. It became a bit of fun and we all appreciated meeting a tree so majestic.

Too soon for my liking we were nearing home, although Sami was ticking off the days with growing relief and making no bones about how he felt. Finally we navigated a narrow track up the Back Table of Table Mountain, having secured special permission to enter the national park with our vehicles, arriving to a heroes' homecoming.

Choked with emotion, I scanned the cheering faces. There was my daughter Tammy, Adelle's family who embrace me as their own, our Toyota benefactor Roger Houghton, media guests and so many other well-wishers. My heart was bursting. We've done it. We were home!

Sadly a wall still separated Sami and I, although I heard afterwards that he'd confided that he'd learned something from each of us – Adelle's contribution a demonstrable love and compassion for animals, while mine was courage.

We'd achieved everything we'd set out to do, although I felt a sadness that I had failed to unify us all. I have since realized that I should have communicated more effectively and been more reassuring, especially in danger zones.

What would have been ideal would have been an open-hearted and non-judge-mental Findhorn-style sharing each morning where we could have expressed our hopes and fears.

Instead of thinking that everyone should simply get on with their appointed job, I could have been more caring and inclusive.

At Findhorn it is routine to start each day with staff members sitting in a circle and saying how they are feeling, while being honest about any anxieties. If we had done this during the expedition it would have dispelled so many tensions and led to greater trust and understanding.

More than a year later I met Sami again at a function and I asked if he'd join me on another expedition – and it feels good to know I meant it. He did a fine job and was a teacher to me, mirroring my own shortcomings.

CHAPTER SEVENTEEN

NOTHING IS IMPOSSIBLE

Nimble thought can jump both sea and land.
– **WILLIAM SHAKESPEARE,** PLAYWRIGHT

Nothing is impossible, if you truly believe it, having complete faith in the universe.

This powerful understanding has served me well and ever since my first ascent of Kilimanjaro I've practised a form of visualisation where I picture successful outcomes, like seeing myself standing on the summit of Uhuru Peak, exhilarated and uplifted. What you focus on becomes your reality, so I try to make it positive and joyful.

Increasingly I've also attempted to see the gift in every situation, reminding myself to ask the question: "What is the lesson?"

So I didn't burst out laughing at the seeming absurdity of it when I received the call: "How would you like to lead an overland expedition from China to South Africa?" Was this a joke?

Apparently not and even the disconcerting news that it would be in cheap Chinese vehicles didn't frighten me off, although my fear of failure did raise its ugly head. "Sure, I'd love to," I replied, despite some serious misgivings. Would this be a pilgrimage in the footsteps of ancient explorers and religious scholars or just another face to the rampant consumerism that is our modern faith? Would my passion for adventure override issues of integrity?

Having witnessed the systematic stripping of the planet's resources and rape of the rainforests, I felt deeply uneasy about a partnership with the Chinese, knowing their ruthless expansionism plans. I was also painfully aware that China has been flooding the market with often inferior products … a brief image flashed into my mind of a landscape littered with bits of broken car, my expedition stranded and egg all over my egotistical face. I'd never failed as an expedition guide and certainly didn't want to now.

There were so many things that could go wrong: mechanical failures, immovable bureaucracy, an ambush by bandits, getting stranded in a quagmire or succumbing to insurmountable traction problems in the ice and snow of the high Himalayas.

Once I wakened at 3am in a sweat, thinking: "You're crazy. You are attempting to take four budget two-wheel-drive vehicles from China to Cape Point along a route that has defeated many a rugged 4x4. Why?"

I debated the issues internally and realized that what was to become Chana Trax 2007 – a massively ambitious 21,000 km, 12-country overland adventure – was a magnificent opportunity to leave my prejudices at home and interact with people from vastly different backgrounds. It would be a chance to follow in the camel tracks of merchants, explorers, monks and scholars who have trod the legendary Silk Road for more than 2000 years.

It was also an opportunity to put into practice the painful lessons learned on previous expeditions and especially my Timbuktu epic when I'd been at the epicentre of serious conflict within the team. I vowed that this time it would be a joyful experience for all.

And whatever happened, I'd pour out heart and soul to readers of *Odyssey Magazine*, a pioneering holistic lifestyle publication born out of a visit to Cape Town from Findhorn's Peter and Eileen Caddy in 1977.

Two days before leaving I dropped into *Odyssey's* offices and Chris and Silke Erasmus insisted: "This you have got to see," handing me a copy of the film, *The Secret*.

The message turned out to be entirely familiar and confirmation of my strategy, although I'd never had the techniques spelt out so logically and eloquently.

The great secret of life is the law of attraction, which says like attracts like. As you think thoughts, they are sent out into the universe, and they magnetically attract all like things that are on the same frequency. So, logically, if you want to change anything in your life, change your thoughts. What you focus on will become your reality. Bingo!

I decide to create a safe bubble for the expedition to travel in, focussing my thoughts and prayers on the success and safety of the mission. I visualized safe passage through Oman, where a cyclone had claimed many lives, and through Yemen where tourists were murdered both ahead and behind us.

Reaching Djibouti and the African continent, I visualized the nightmare of appalling dirt tracks through armed bandit country in northern Kenya finally ending. Fast forward another few days and I see our happy little band arriving safely at the car company's local headquarters in Johannesburg.

Did it work? And what other forces were at play? I later learned that many prayers were said for us, with blessings asked for the Chana Trax project before the green light was finally given by the company's devoutly Christian management in South Africa.

I'm not sure what they would have thought of the incense I lit at a Buddhist temple in China at the start of the epic, or the travelling Buddha statuette mounted to my car's dashboard. But I'm grateful for blessings from whatever sources. I also relished priceless moments of quiet meditation in churches, mosques and temples, although my favourite place of worship is invariably anywhere in nature where I can marvel at the beauty of creation.

The 86-day odyssey was amazing and mostly joyful thanks to the wonderful core team of like-minded souls: PR and marketing man Christo Kruger, project manager Corinna Howard, Adelle, mechanic Andries Kruger and paramedic Hugh Price-Hughes.

Admittedly I didn't much like the deviousness of our Chinese host company, sometimes squirming at the idea that I was a willing part of their overall propaganda machine.

I was also painfully aware that the project's ecological footprint was huge, journalists and members of the Chana marketing team flying in and out to join us for legs of the epic adventure. But I'd like to think everybody was richer for the experience, with broader perspectives.

I'm also pleased that the expedition showcased a solution to our transport needs based on an affordable and utilitarian minimalism, rather than our usual obsessive craving for power, luxury and technological superiority. When is more just too much?

And even the most affluent tourist would be hard pressed to replicate what we were paid to do.

Our journey started in bustling Chongqing, the most populous city in the world with 32 million souls, the mayoral send-off including red carpets, speeches, TV cameras, fireworks and a soaking rain that seemed especially auspicious.

Contrasts were astonishing, ranging from travelling below sea-level through one of the lowest spots in the world in the Turpan Depression to the Khunjerab Pass between China and Pakistan that is the planet's highest paved border crossing. My GPS registered 4,733 metres.

Along the way we traversed the endless monotony of the pitiless Gobi and Taklamakan Deserts before entering breathtaking snow-capped mountain scenery and arriving at the roof of the world where the Himalayas meet the Karakoram and Hindu Kush ranges. It is easy to believe that God lives here amid all this beauty, and to understand the enduring magnetic pull to spiritual pilgrims.

We passed through the Great Wall which remains a towering feat of engineering, especially when you consider it was initiated more than 2,000 years ago and snakes through deserts, hills and forests over thousands of kilometres. Arguably the greatest national icon anywhere, it is symbolic of China's sense of vulnerability. One suspects that that same sense of threat drives the country's avarice for resources today.

The Wall survives where a number of monuments don't; the country's tortured past including the notorious Cultural Revolution of the 1960s when Chairman Mao called on the masses to abolish all distinctions between classes and manual and intellectual work. Remnants of the past were smashed, among them many superb temples.

Now there is a delicious irony in the cheap Mickey Mouse-style Mao watches selling in souvenir shops.

Talk to young Chinese about Tian'an Men Square, where a call for political reform and an end to corruption was brutally suppressed in 1989, claiming many lives, and they don't know what really happened. "You know more than we do," I was told.

Of all the cities, X'ian was a favourite. It is the western starting point of the Silk Road and its greatest historical treasure is the Terra Cotta Army of more than 7,000 life-like soldiers and horses.

Created by the first emperor in Chinese history, the mute army was intended to smooth his passage in the afterlife, his massive sense of self-importance rivalling that of the pharaohs in Egypt's Valley of the Kings.

Think what you might of the man, it is remarkable to see such detailed work on such a grand scale, the terra cotta soldiers all featuring individual faces and expressions.

It was here that former US president Bill Clinton met the humble farmer who first discovered the remarkable collection and asked for his autograph. It turned out that he could neither read nor write, and was hugely embarrassed by his predicament.

Thanks to some intensive tutoring, he was able to sign the souvenir book I bought with a grand flourish.

It was also in X'ian that the monk Xuanzang returned from India with sutras that are housed in the Great Goose Pagoda, playing a part in the gradual spread of Buddhism eastwards through China to Japan around 600 CE.

Along our route we encountered many reminders of those early pilgrims, and none more intriguing than at the Mogao Grottos at Duanhuang, that are commonly known as the 'Thousand Buddha Caves.' The world heritage site today boasts 492 surviving caves, thousands of sculptures and superb religious murals that would stretch 45 km if linked together. It was so fascinating I wished I could have stayed days longer.

In the town of Dunhuang we drank beer in the market and were serenaded by troubadours who spoke not a word of English, but did a convincing and wildly popular rendition of Auld Lang Syne.

The language challenge raised its head often, but no more embarrassingly than when I went for a massage at a hotel and was lying naked under a towel, eyes closed, when a very attractive naked woman walked in and began fondling my penis. I protested and she seemed to think this was part of the game, climbing on top of me and attempting to get me steamed up. I'd booked a massage and bought a hooker.

Eventually my irritation got through and she left, a burly guy immediately appearing in her place. "Oh my God, they think I'm gay," I thought, but he kept his clothes on and turned out to be an excellent masseur.

At around midnight there was a knock on the door to the room I was sharing with Adelle and I opened it to the same young woman, this time with her clothes on at least. Some people can't take 'No' for an answer.

Adelle Horler with soldiers in Cameroon. Armed escorts were a feature in many countries we explored on our expeditions

Driving over the Khunjerab Pass I was thrilled to at last be free of my Chinese handlers and able to run the expedition my way, although we had a succession of heavily armed Pakistani police escorts and were confined to our hotel in Sukkur, because of fears that a protest march might turn violent .

Locals everywhere were friendly and curious, even when our keepers were high-handed in keeping them apart from us. Strolling in a street market we were protected by members of an elite task force wearing black 'No Fear' shirts. We felt especially awkward when we visited a tomb of deep significance to local Muslims and our armed keepers formed a human shield. Perhaps we shouldn't have been there at all, as we were more tourists than pilgrims.

I wonder what it would be like today in the aftermath of the murder of Osama Bin Laden. Probably a lot more sensitive.

The bedlam of Karachi kamikaze traffic marked the end of the first leg of our journey, our four cars being loaded into containers for a sea journey to the United Arab Emirates and Dubai, the world's biggest shopping mall and a towering glass and steel monument to glitzy materialism and the concept of more, bigger and better. Have all spiritual values been sacrificed on the altar of consumerism?

Driving to neighbouring Oman was heartening indeed, especially as the Sultanate was responding with great pride and sensitivity to the cyclone that claimed hundreds of lives and wreaked incredible havoc days earlier. A wonderful sense of caring community prevailed and I was deeply impressed by the people.

Reaching the border with Yemen we marvelled at how much could change so soon. Does it all come down to attitude and commitment?

Gone were the high ideals and obsessive cleanliness, the border officials immediately trying to scam us, while the presence of so many weapons in civilian hands was alarming. And from around 2pm it seemed that most of the adult male population was increasingly stoned as they chewed the narcotic leaf of the qat plant, one cheek ballooning like a ball as they kept adding to the wad of green gunge.

Yemen often delights with its scenic beauty and ancient history, but it is dirty and feels dangerously unstable.

At Al Mukalla we'd been looking forward to the coast drive south to Aden, when we received a late-night warning of widespread unrest and dissidents promising to kidnap foreigners to use as bargaining tools with the government. Thanks, but no thanks.

So we re-routed through spectacular mountain desert scenery that could have been straight out of the Bible, getting really excited when we realised that we would pass the temple of the legendary Queen of Sheba which was apparently built in the 10th century BCE.

Sadly it is in the province of Marib, a terrorist stronghold near a US-controlled oilfield, where security is intense – we spotted tank, armoured car and artillery placements and were told stopping would be lunacy.

Our little convoy was only permitted passage in the company of a camouflage-painted pickup with a huge machine-gun mounted on the back.

We briefly glimpsed the temple while travelling virtually at maximum speed, lamenting the unhappy collision of beliefs that have fanned the flames for religious fundamentalists.

Days later we were shocked by headlines that a suspected Al Qaeda suicide bomber had killed 10 Spanish tourists on a visit to the same temple, imagining the horror of the scene and trying to visualize the pain that would drive a person to such an awful deed.

Leaving Yemen there was a sense of gratitude that we'd enjoyed kindness and safe passage, but also joy that the next seven countries and 8,000 km would be through Africa, our eventual homecoming being everything we could wish for.

CHAPTER EIGHTEEN

MOTHER GODDESS
OF THE WORLD

What we get from this adventure is just sheer joy.
And joy is, after all, the end of life.
We do not live to eat and make money.
We eat and make money to be able to enjoy life.
That is what life means and what life is for.

— *GEORGE LEIGH MALLORY*, EVEREST'S MOST FAMOUS FATALITY

Spirituality and nature connectedness are ultimately one and the same and where better to experience both than within the haunting beauty of the high Himalayas.

In 2007, having devoted more than a year to helping plan and lead the first motorised overland expedition from China to Cape Town, I knew without doubt that I must answer a deep yearning to meet Chomolungma, the mountain colossus known to Tibetans as the Mother Goddess of the World.

An historic drive halfway around the world had included the legendary Silk Road from China to Pakistan and the highpoint – figuratively and literally for me – was the spectacular meeting point of the Earth's three great mountain ranges: the Himalayas, Karakoram and Hindu Kush. But tantalisingly hidden from view was a jewel in the crown, Mount Everest herself.

Although mesmerized by the scale and magnificence of the towering peaks, I suddenly lamented the deadline urgencies of this pioneering expedition, recognising that even the modest speed of our four budget Chinese vehicles was too fast. To put my life into perspective and reappraise where I was going I needed to slow down to pilgrim walking pace.

I vowed to return within weeks and trek through Nepal to Everest Base Camp, perhaps as a precursor to seeing the world from its summit, conveniently ignoring the fact that more than 200 unrecovered bodies are frozen monuments to the mortality and vulnerability of even the most skilled climbers.

"If you wish to climb Everest you must be prepared to never see your daughters again," Adelle warned, homing in on the thing most likely to get my attention. It was water off a duck's back. All my expeditions had been successful and dying on a mountain wasn't in the script I'd written for a life that has always seemed charmed.

Adelle had also argued that simply being on the mountain is enough. It isn't always necessary to view life from the summit. Yeah, yeah!

While I'd secretly cherished the ambition to climb Everest, my Nepalese adventure was a month-long look-see, reaching Base Camp via a 16-day hike that would immerse me in the Tibetan Buddhist culture of the region and also take in the beautiful turquoise Gokyu lakes and include a trek over the daunting Cho La Pass.

At just 5,364 metres how tough could Base Camp be? Having twice stood on the 5,895 metres summit of Kilimanjaro in the preceding three years, as well as hiking the Inca Trail in Peru, I wasn't too worried, even as a former asthmatic who has known the terror of struggling to breathe.

I was ecstatic about the journey and wrote in *Odyssey Magazine*:

"God lives in the high mountains of the Himalayas of Nepal.

The reminders of our precious connection to the Divine are to be found everywhere from the gaily fluttering Buddhist prayer flags welcoming pilgrims, to the ancient monasteries, stone altars and carved rock tablets that speak of a centuries-old devotion and reverence for life.

Even the cheerful clinking of yak bells seems somehow to carry special messages, perhaps reinforcing the mantras of devoted monks and their time-honoured chants: 'Om mani padme hum, Om mani padme hum…'

Then, of course, there is the breathtaking scenery itself. Who can fail to be stirred by such awesome landscapes? Each breath of crisp mountain air makes you want to sing with joy and gratitude at such bountiful blessings. Is there any place on Earth more stunning than the Himalayas, or any better spot to be alive?"

Nepal might be one of the poorer countries on the planet but it is blessed with no fewer than eight of the 14 peaks that thrust above 8, 000 metres into the atmosphere, the most famous of which is Everest.

Treading ever higher along rocky Himalayan paths is a boyhood dream come true. Since attending a talk by Sir Edmund Hillary in Durban, and then shyly asking for his autograph, I'd fantasised about standing on the top of the world with no higher place to climb.

I'd read the books of courage, determination and disaster; studied the statistics too. The quest to reach the top of Everest took longer than putting a man on the moon, although by 2007 some 11,000 souls had committed to the ascent, 3,000 of them succeeding – an encouraging success rate of 29%. But the dark side of the statistics is that 207 climbers had also died with many of their bodies preserved by the icy cold where they fell.

Accompanying me were friends Deon Ebersohn, a Cape Town journalist and former motor industry executive, Jen Newenham, an environmental consultant, Nepali guide Dibash Onta and porters Sudip Baral and Rajan Bishowkarma. The trio of locals are a lesson in cheerful optimism, good humour and amazing physical stamina.

Sherpa is the tribal name for the Himalayan people living in the mountains of Nepal and Tibet, rather than a job description, although 'sherpa' is synonymous in the minds of most Westerners with porters of incredible strength and courage who are seemingly immune to the debilitating and potentially lethal effects of Acute Mountain Sickness (AMS).

Nothing could be further from the truth, we discover during a talk by volunteer doctors at a rescue post.

A snap survey of this particular audience reveals that many of the Sherpas are from the Kathmandu Valley or other low-lying areas, and it is a documented fact that they also suffer altitude-related illnesses, although they invariably hide these for fear of losing desperately needed income for their families.

Himalayan trekkers Jen Newenham, Deon Ebersohn and Geoff with Everest in the background

What is verifiable is that the legendary climbing Sherpas have adapted better to altitude, their blood carrying more oxygen than usual. But because of their prolonged exposure to risk while establishing safe routes for paying climbers to follow, and lugging equipment to high camps, they too are crushed in avalanches, fall into crevasses or succumb to extreme exposure.

Perhaps the greatest contemporary local legend was Babu Sherpa who summited Everest 10 times by the age of 36, and spent a record 21 hours on the summit without oxygen, only to fall to his death while apparently taking a photograph at one of the lower camps.

Whatever their genetic makeup, the Sherpas are the real heroes, selflessly devoting their lives to realising the dreams of their clients while supporting their families. For them it is not a recreational pursuit, but a practical necessity.

To the Sherpas mountains are not obstacles to be conquered but living beings to be treated with utmost respect.

Often we felt humbled by the cheeriness of the locals and their reverence for life as they greet strangers with the traditional 'Namaste' that recognises the God within.

It is easy to understand how Edmund Hillary was so touched by his climbing companion Tenzing Norgay Sherpa and the deep spirituality of his people.

Ed, as he was known, is proof of the difference one person can make. He created the Himalayan Trust which established no fewer than 27 schools, two hospitals and 12 clinics in Nepal, as well as piping fresh water to villages, creating airstrips, building bridges over difficult mountain rivers and restoring and maintaining the Sherpas' beloved Buddhist monasteries.

"Achievements are important and I have revelled in a number of good adventures, but far more worthwhile are the tasks I have been able to carry out for my friends in the Himalayas," he said.

As each day unfolds I celebrate my strengthening muscles, feeling the flab fall of me, although I too am touched by AMS, suffering minor headaches, nausea, sleeplessness and loss of appetite. Once I awake with a huge start, feeling panicked and realise that I have momentarily stopped breathing.

A long night stretches ahead of me facing my fears. I was an asthmatic as a child and having my oxygen levels reduced to little more than half by altitude is troubling enough, although nowhere near as scary as the idea of not breathing at all – even for a couple of seconds!

I put my absolute trust in the process of Life, visualize positive outcomes and eventually quieten my fears. Dawn is a magnificent reward, another stunning day making a mockery of my night-time anxieties.

Two books are keeping me company: *Freedom in Exile,* the autobiography of the Dalai Lama and *Left for Dead*, the account of American Beck Weathers and his horrific part in the 1996 tragedy when eight climbers died in a killer storm high on Everest.

I'm tormented by both volumes.

Each day as I trek higher, but always secure in the knowledge that modest lodgings and good food await me, I think of the Tibetan exiles who continue to flee the Chinese occupation and religious persecution in their own country.

Many walk in fear for days and weeks, often while poorly equipped for high-altitude conditions. Many are monks and nuns, while a number of the freedom-seekers are children as young as six or seven.

Their most usual destination is Dharamsala, home of the Dalai Lama and Tibetan government-in-exile in India, although exiles also enter Nepal, among them traders who cross the border illegally to sell their wares in settlements like Namche Bazar and Tengboche.

Outside the famous Tengboche monastery I watch monks bartering with Tibetans who have walked for several days to sell their cheap Chinese-made clothing. A story is circulating of seven of their kin shot dead recently by Chinese border guards and one has great empathy for people forced to take such risks for a few Rupees.

In contrast with the human rights abuses across the border, the Buddhist message of love, peace and respect for all life is everywhere around us. Many of the places we stay in feature shrines and posters of His Holiness, the Dalai Lama, along with scenes from Tibet. Some of our hosts are of proudly Tibetan origin.

It seems especially sad that genocide, torture and extreme religious persecution have been practiced on a formerly peace-loving nation, and I'm struck by the gentleness of all who I meet. Not once during my trek do I hear a local voice raised in anger or recrimination, although we do have to endure one obnoxiously loud American woman trekker and a group of drunken Koreans who show no respect for their fellow travellers.

Is it karma that causes the Koreans to miss their international flight out of Kathmandu? We try not to gloat.

Thinking of the brutality of the Chinese towards the Tibetans, who are now a minority race in their own country, I'm reminded of the Dalai Lama's comment that his Chinese brothers and sisters are not bad people, but just people behaving badly.

Walking for 16 days allows plenty of time for introspection, along with a deep appreciation for the opportunity to step back in time to an almost medieval lifestyle. Not once do I see any form of motorised transport or even a wheel: no cars, motorcycles, bicycles or wheelbarrows in sight. Instead everything is carried on the backs of humans, yaks and the dzopkios that are a cross between a yak and a cow.

We marvel at the realisation that we are witnessing a hotel being carried into the Himalayas in pieces, which also explains why the sound-deadening is so abysmal in the overnight hostelries – how could it be otherwise with lightweight plywood panels for walls!

Seemingly small things like a hot shower are really appreciated. In Kathmandu a bottle of mineral water costs 15 Rupees, the price soaring twenty-fold in the remoter regions of the Himalayas. And while a good meal is really cheap, a hot shower will cost progressively more the closer you get to Base Camp.

Often the water has to be carried considerable distance and then heated using dried yak dung. So nothing is easy!

Electricity is also a precious commodity, the meagre illumination during our overnight stays invariably provided by solar panels, and then only when there have been a few hours of sunlight.

Life is simple but joyful.

As a pilgrim I have all I could wish for, my essentials including a battery-powered head torch, down sleeping bag, warm trekking clothes, an inquiring mind and a keen sense of humour.

We encounter mist, rain, sleet, snow and biting winds, but on the days when it really matters we celebrate clear sunny views of Everest and other legendary peaks like Nuptse, Lhotse and Ama Dablam.

Highlights include the breathtaking panorama from Goko Ri across a wide glacier towards Everest, as well as the ascent of Cho La Pass in deteriorating weather conditions. It is one of the toughest hikes I've yet experienced and constantly fraught with the danger of slipping on ice or snow-covered rocks and boulders. The Pass was closed just before our arrival, and again after the brief window of opportunity with which we were blessed before fresh snowstorms.

On the top of Cho La I was staggering with exhaustion as I trudged through deep snow in the gloom, slipping and falling more than once. But my spirits soared and I felt so incredibly alive – this is the kind of dramatic Himalayan landscape I'd dreamed of and the sort of physical challenge I relish.

The guidebooks and some friends had warned me that Base Camp might be an anti-climax, lacking a meaningful view of Everest. But I was energized and exhilarated by the experience of trekking along the edge of the Khumbu Icefall and Glacier, at last coming face-to-face with that giant conveyer belt of rock and ice that forms one of the daunting obstacles to any summit attempt.

Fulfilling a lifelong dream to meet Everest, the Mother Goddess of the World

The main weather window happens in May each year, allowing a few teams a crack at the top when the notorious jetstream is not howling off the summit at up to 250 km/h. We reach Base Camp in sunshine on October 11 to find Thailand's first Everest bid in progress with the team planning to be there for three months.

Depending on your viewpoint this could be the ultimate life-changing gift, or your worst nightmare in the bleakest and most hostile environment imaginable.

I love every precious second and am stirred by the aliveness of the scene, drawing a deep breath every time I hear the cracking and crunching of the moving glacier, or the roar of an avalanche exploding from the high peaks.

I volunteer a silent prayer of thanks for being here in this remarkable landscape, and more especially for all my bountiful blessings. I've grateful for the epiphany and opening of my heart chakra with the dazzling realisation that nothing is more important than my daughters Tammy and Bonnie and others so dear to me.

Willi Unsoeld, one of the first American team to summit, put it aptly: "You've climbed the highest mountain in the world. What's left? It's all downhill from there. You've got to set your sights on something higher than Everest."

I have - I'd rather hug my loved ones again than experience the unbelievable adrenaline-rush of standing on the very top of this magnificent world of ours. But I can dream can't I?

CHAPTER NINETEEN

ANIMAL WHISPERS

*The greatness of a nation and its moral progress
can be judged by the way its animals are treated.*
— *MAHATMA GANDHI,* HUMANITARIAN

The wheel seems to be turning full circle when it comes to acceptance of the idea of interspecies communication.

What the First People of the planet, among them the San Bushmen, Aborigines and Native Americans, routinely understood and embraced is finding favour in the modern mainstream and I guess we can thank Hollywood for popularising the idea of interspecies communication, especially in the wake of wide-screen movie blockbusters like *Avatar* and *Alice in Wonderland*.

But how ironic that humanity's disconnection from Nature is so pervasive that many of us only entertain the possibility of other levels of perception – and communication - while sitting indoors and wearing 3D glasses!

Of course, interspecies communication isn't new to movie-makers and more than any other film it was *The Horse Whisperer* of 1998 that lent credibility to the concept as our celluloid hero Tom Booker, played by Robert Redford, helped heal a seriously injured young girl and her psychologically-scarred horse. How many of us were touched by that story?

Was it fact or fancy? Can some of us really communicate with animals?

Somehow the idea of inter-species communication never seemed far-fetched to me, perhaps because I'd grown up with my mother's imaginative story-telling and been enthralled by her collection of animal stories for children.

It was contained in a book entitled *Tales from the Baobab Tree* and I never questioned the immense wisdom of that elephantine baobab, then or now. Why would the mighty African baobab not enrich us with the tales of the amazing happenings beneath its vast spreading branches through the centuries? And if a tree could speak; why not other creatures great and small: why not all of nature?

I became obsessed with the possibility, finally deciding to put it to the test during my regular hike up Lion's Head, one of Cape Town's most rewarding walks with the gift of panoramic views of the city and Table Mountain looming alongside. I vowed that today I'd communicate directly with nature.

But how? And what creature would be the target of my first experiment? Reaching the summit I looked around and was delighted to see I had all this magnificence to myself, with not another human in sight. Scanning the rocky landscape I spotted a lizard innocently sunning itself on a rock some distance away. Why not. I quieted my mind and tried to beam good vibes in its direction. How do you introduce yourself to a reptile? Do you say: 'Hello Lizard. My name is Geoff.' No, that wouldn't work.

Instead I attempted to silently convey my deep love of the natural world and all creatures (conveniently overlooking an aversion to flies, fleas, mosquitoes, midges and blood-sucking ticks). My telepathic message was simple: I love all of creation and wish to somehow serve, either as a self-appointed ecological activist or simply as a humble human with no wish to dominate or conquer the natural world. I tried to convey immense gratitude to the lizard for the fact of its existence and interconnectedness in the web of life.

Lizard was suddenly galvanised into action. Darting forward, it hopped onto and over rocks, sometimes momentarily disappearing from view, as it raced towards me in a series of agile reptilian spurts. I'd taken off my trainers and socks, and was enjoying the sun on my skin. Imagine my surprise when it began nibbling my toes.

I was astonished. This had never happened before. Were we somehow communicating?

I felt elated, returning the next day to the same spot. It happened again, this time with a different species of lizard. Today's representative of the reptile kingdom was bigger and I felt a twinge of anxiety when it came scurrying over and bit my big toe rather harder than I would have liked. I resisted the urge to pull my foot back and discourage the dialogue.

Something was happening between me and the world of nature. Yay!

Many other contacts have followed since; my encounters involving other lizards along with bats, eagles, baboons, whales, elephants and even tiny mice scuttling unseen around my sleeping bag in the dark.

My research had reminded me that the San Bushmen and other indigenous peoples have always insisted that they could communicate with the natural world around them. But could we modern humans do the same?

I conducted a random survey, expecting ridicule, and was surprised by how many people are emphatic that not only is it possible, but desirable and important to the future well-being of the planet and all its inhabitants. And I encountered a number of wildlife and conservation professionals who either practice forms of inter-species communication or routinely call in an animal whisperer.

Interestingly some birders are beginning to see it as a way to connect with what the birds are saying, appreciating that our feathered friends are the journalists of the bush with a story to tell anybody who stops to listen.

I increasingly felt a kinship with the wild creatures I was meeting but I can't say I really understood what was going on or what, if anything, was being said.

I needed an interpreter.

Meeting South African training facilitator Anna Breytenbach was synchronicity at work and I signed up for three of her weekend workshops. The fact that she was beautiful as well made the research even more compelling. Hey Geoff, don't go falling in love with her!

"Animal communication is not a gift," the lovely Anna assured me. "It is a natural ability that everybody has and is simply a matter of getting in touch with our intuition and accessing something that isn't part of our everyday five-sensory reality.

"The First People and indigenous tribes like the San Bushmen and Native Americans were easily able to communicate telepathically with all of nature and didn't consider this unusual.

"Every person in the tribe had the ability to connect in non five-sensory ways with their surroundings; to know from the animals where they were, which was a good animal to hunt, or which plants would be medicinal, toxic or nourishing."

While formalised interspecies communication courses are relatively new to many countries, the benefits are increasingly being appreciated by wildlife managers, conservation officials, environmentalists and veterinarians.

Anna is one of a handful of fulltime communicators in Africa, conducting workshops and consulting with organisations as diverse as The Global White Lion Protection Trust, Jukani Predator Sanctuary, Baboon Matters, Monkeyland and CapeCROW (Centre for the Rehabilitation of Wildlife).

"I'm not teaching people anything new," she says. "I'm merely helping them remember what's already within them and I think that it's important to again experience a deep connectedness with nature. When we experience a direct empathetic connection with another being we're much more inclined to understand the perspective of that animal and the challenges it faces, particularly at the hands of humans and what we are doing to this planet."

"Interspecies communication brings about mutual understanding and respect along with the possibility of co-creating solutions for even the most tricky situations where wildlife and humans come into conflict."

My own curiosity about the subject had again been aroused when Adelle and I faced possible death after being charged by eight elephants in a camp bordering

Animal whisperer Anna Breytenbach at Findhorn with Dorothy Maclean

Zambia's South Luangwa National Park. Terrified, we hid behind a tree and with a determination born of pure terror I attempted to communicate telepathically that I meant no harm – and have no idea if the message was received.

So it was a somewhat surreal moment when I found myself surrounded by a dozen of these giants at the Knysna Elephant Park during a workshop with Anna.

The last time I'd been this close my life hung in the balance, although this time the atmosphere was benign, one pachyderm reaching out a trunk and gently exploring me.

Anna was relaxed so I took my cue from her. Be calm and unconditionally loving.

She says the same techniques apply whether connecting with wild animals or domestic or habituated ones. Often her services are called upon to calm a wild creature that has been rescued or is being rehabilitated.

"In these situations wild animals are incredibly stressed at suddenly being in confined surroundings with all the human noises of people, cars and machinery."

Her role then is to calm the animal with reassurances that the people are there to help, while explaining what is required of them, particularly if medical intervention is necessary.

In the wilds communicators can assist by warning of impending danger like the presence of poachers and can even suggest – through mental imagery – possible safe escape routes.

With rewilding programmes such as the reintroduction of captive white lions into a natural environment it is also useful to convey the dangers of targeting a prey species like a giraffe which could inflict a devastating kick to a naïve predator. This involves sending clear and graphic telepathic images of the injuries that could result.

"The things I would communicate with wild animals about if they are happily going about their own business in the natural environment would be about their lifestyles. It is a great opportunity to find out what it is like to be in those paws."

"So I might ask the leopard 'how does it feel to be dragging an antelope kill up the tree?' The response I'll get is a very real feeling within my own body of that power, strength and latent potential."

"I might ask a sleeping lion how it is experiencing its body and its surroundings and feel this fantastic, absolute relaxation as if I'm having a deep meditation myself."

"And if I was asking one of the antelope species about its favourite food the answer might be a mental image of the animal stretching its neck up to browse off a particular bush or a taste in my own mouth of the acidity of that particular leaf."

Anna maintains that communicators can be especially helpful in enhancing relationships between medical professionals and their animal patients, be they wild or otherwise. "For example, vets can find out directly – from the horse's mouth, so to speak – what the animal's experience of their pain or discomfort is; where in the body it occurs; what might have caused it; and even what might make it better."

"This is immensely helpful to medical professionals who otherwise have to rely on observation and other diagnostic measures alone."

During the workshop I teamed up with another participant who I'd never met before and we exchanged photographs of dogs that we are close to, my picture featuring Adelle's faithful companion, a fabulous Border collie called Ruby who I adore.

Within minutes my workshop partner reported a mental image of Ruby behind a wooden fence alongside a river, which was 95% accurate, the collie living next to a vast wetland.

I felt slightly foolish and very unsure of myself when it was my turn to tap into my intuition. I described a world viewed from knee-height – the height of a medium-sized dog. Looking up I saw a colony of weavers' nests in trees overhead and the confirmation was instant. "Yes, the dog is fascinated by the birds in the back garden."

Then I ventured another perception: "Your dog has a red, plastic feeding bowl?"

Bingo. Somehow, with the help of a photograph clearly showing her dog's eyes, I was communicating telepathically.

How could this be?

Anna explains: "Animals communicate through physical action (body language), their own complex languages (vocalisation) and telepathy. People receive the messages to the degree that they are listening and can tune in, like twirling the dials of an old radio, to be on the same energetic wavelength.

"Telepathic communication involves the direct transmission of feelings, intentions, thoughts, mental images, emotions, impressions and pure knowing.

"The actual mechanism for this lies firmly in the field of quantum physics. Thoughts and emotions generate an electromagnetic consequence in the brain, and these frequencies are available for perceiving – by scientific equipment or our own more complex receiving device, the mind."

Anna admits that she was deeply sceptical when she first encountered the concept of animal communications while working as an IT professional in the United States.

Geoff communicating with elephants

"My passion had always been wildlife and Nature and I decided to do tracking training with the Wilderness Awareness School, outside Seattle. Because I grew up in South Africa I didn't know a thing about the North American animals. I didn't know how to interpret the footprints I was seeing in the sand. Even though I could recognise that the animal had four toes, for example, I had no idea what might have created those footprints.

"My instructors told me simply to sit with the tracks and see what impressions came my way. When I closed my eyes I would get mental flashes – brief images of various animal faces or bodies. This happened with a coyote's tracks, and with a mink, neither of which animals I had ever encountered. But when I described my mental visions my instructors confirmed that those animals had indeed left those tracks.

"I was highly sceptical. My logical and very ordinary upbringing couldn't account for this way of knowing something. At first I thought it was purely a fluke, a coincidence or a lucky guess."

While continuing her day job, she studied through the respected Assisi International Animal Institute which operates from the basic premise that all animals – human and non-human – are sentient beings and can express their intelligence in various ways and can be communicated with.

Numerous case studies were conducted in a way in which the results could be validated, finally convincing Anna that what she was experiencing was real.

I'm equally certain that I have begun an important two-way dialogue although I feel like an infant struggling to mouth its first words.

On a mountaintop I meet a large male baboon with signs of some recent injuries. I sit quietly and communicate love and respect. He chooses to sit near me, casting periodic glances in my direction, and I suddenly feel a wave of loneliness engulfing me as I long for the company, touch and grooming of the troop.

I subsequently discover the reasons for his solitary presence. He is an ageing former alpha male of a local troop of baboons that has been driven out by a younger and stronger rival.

I feel certain I've established a direct empathetic connection and am unsurprised when we meet again a couple of mornings later and share a companionable silence, both quietly appreciating our lofty viewpoint and the growing warmth of the sun. No words are necessary.

Meeting baboons somehow reminds me of our responsibilities as the dominant species on the planet, also helping me to reconnect with the natural world. It is a reminder that connecting is not only about cellphones, emails and the Internet, but the need to get in touch with our humanity again.

Time in the company of wild creatures can be a life-changing gift.

CHAPTER TWENTY

GIANT LEAP OF FAITH

Breathe. Let go.
And remind yourself that this very moment
is the only one you know you have for sure.
— *OPRAH WINFREY*, TV TALKSHOW HOST

Divinity has many faces and on that chilly morning, when I stood nervously on the cliff-edge alongside Maletsunyane Falls in the African kingdom of Lesotho, I said a silent prayer for the safety of us all, and then felt a shadow passing over me. I looked up to see a magnificent Verreaux's Eagle soaring above.

It seemed almost too perfect, as if Hollywood had scripted the day, the black eagle with its distinctive panels of white in the wings, rocking gently and gliding on a thermal above us alongside one of Africa's great waterfalls.

It was a sign: the moment was blessed and each of us would extract from the day exactly what we needed.

A great calm came over me, feelings of incredible gratitude blending with the joy of being totally alive with all my senses heightened. I felt awed by the abundance of my blessings, running through a mental checklist of things for which I was hugely grateful, among them the love and inspiration of my daughters Bonnie and Tammy, and the awesome gift of this day of high adventure in the company of Inga Hendriks, a very special person in my life, and two new friends.

Months of planning had brought us to this time and place, for today we'd brave the world's highest single-drop commercial abseil, hopefully helping Inga confront and conquer her terror of heights.

She's taught me not to take myself too seriously, to laugh at life and to recapture that sense of spontaneous fun that children are so good at.

Could I repay those precious gifts by holding up a mirror to the amazing and incredibly modest Inga I see? Could I help her appreciate her true worth and huge potential? Perhaps stepping over this cliff would be a step in the right direction.

Fear, I'd reminded myself earlier to no avail, was simply an acronym for False Evidence Appearing Real. Now those apprehensions, and a night haunted by sleeplessness and absurd imaginings, seemed ridiculous.

All the inevitable 'what if' questions had surfaced in the dark hours. What if the rope jammed in the mechanism, or snagged on a rock? Or worse, what if the rope snapped, sending one of us plummeting 204 metres to the rocks below! (Actually there's a second safety line, so that couldn't happen).

Funnily enough, with more than 30 abseils behind me, I knew the risks were minimal and worried more about Inga, wondering if I'd been unfair to coax her into confronting her demons in such dramatic style. Was it simply my ego that had made me recommend the world's longest abseil for her baptism?

She was remarkable, though, proving that we are all capable of more than we imagine. The day before our hosts at Semonkong Lodge had rightly insisted that we tackle three much smaller abseils on a nearby cliff to hone our techniques and familiarise ourselves with the equipment and especially a device known ominously as The Rack. (It's a clever metal gadget that allows the abseiler to control the speed of descent while dissipating the heat generated by more than 200 metres of rope passing through its friction mechanisms).

Confronting the first drop of 25 metres, Inga decided the madness would end right there. "I've changed my mind," she informed local adventure guide Felix Sebilo. "I'm not going to do it!

"Felix seemed sad at the news and looked deeply into my eyes. I felt as if I was disappointing him, and he gently encouraged me to carry on. I realise now that he could sell ice to Eskimos – or an abseil to an Inga. I stepped backwards over the edge. It was terrifying and horrible."

She repeated the exercise three times that day, and once in the night confided to me in a very small voice: "I'm so scared."

The next morning it was obvious that she was still frightened, but Inga the award-winning photographer had surfaced with a grim resolve. "I'm going first and then I'll photograph the rest of you coming down from my vantage point at the bottom of the gorge," she announced firmly. Yes Sir!

I crawled to the edge of the cliff and peered over, feeling my gut churn at the enormity of what she was doing. I felt a moment of panic. What was she feeling? Her yellow-helmeted figure was getting smaller and smaller and melting into the vast landscape of cliffs and thundering spray until I could barely see her. Was she experiencing heaven or hell?

After an agony of waiting it was my turn. I tried to grin reassuringly at my friends Cindy May, a journalist, and Caleb, her paramedic hubby, who were looking tense and introspective. Hopefully we wouldn't need Caleb's services.

I levered myself backwards with guidance from Felix and almost immediately found myself spiralling on the end of the rope. It was both deeply disconcerting and breathtakingly beautiful. Had I ever witnessed a scene to top this one, I mused?

Feelings of love and gratitude swamped me and I grinned delightedly at the idea of so many people elsewhere toiling behind their office desks while I was having the time of my life.

I also pondered the words of my host Jonathan Halse, who'd explained: "The abseil brings you down to earth. You are just a yellow dot hanging next to these giant cliffs that are millions of years old. It gives a sense of scale and a measure of your importance in the scheme of things."

Inga Hendriks in party mood. She confronted her fear of heights with the worlds's highest commercial abseil

I discovered that just when you are feeling really confident the last section of the abseil throws up fresh challenges as you are immersed in flying spray, the temperature plummeting and the rocks becoming very, very slippery. Dangerously slippery!

I was forced to temper my exuberance, dramatically slowing the pace and placing each foot tentatively against the slick cliff face as I continued to balance my descent. It was tricky and I was torn between wishing to stretch out each precious adrenaline-charged second and wanting to get it over and plant my feet solidly on terra firma again.

Touching down at the end of my 15-minute leap of faith I felt like the airline commander who'd performed the perfect landing. I was the 736th person to earn a certificate for a feat ratified as a Guinness World Record.

Cindy May and Caleb followed and I worried why she was going so slowly, taking 33 agonising minutes. But her sodden grin on landing was all joy and adrenaline.

"Beauty is such a subjective thing, but I always find myself at a loss for words, and sometimes actions, when faced with it in the extreme," Cindy May admitted breathlessly.

Afterwards we all hugged delightedly, although it was some days before Inga had the perspective to describe her feelings. "At first I merely thought: 'I've done it,' she said. Then later, 'Wow … I've done it!'

"Expressions like 'life-changing' came to mind but they sounded too cheesy to verbalize. The experience has made me more confident though. I feel good about myself and know now that I can do other things that still scare me.

"With the benefit of hindsight it was perfectly safe and I should have enjoyed it more. I'd like to do the abseil again and really enjoy the experience, rather than being so scared.

"Meanwhile I have this other great fear to consider … spiders!" Atta Girl … Inga you know you can do it!

CHAPTER TWENTY ONE

OPERATION SMILE

Only those who have learned the power of sincere and selfless
contribution experience Life's deepest joy: true fulfilment.
— *ANTHONY ROBBINS,* AUTHOR AND PEAK PERFORMANCE STRATEGIST

It was in a tiny jail cell on Robben Island that I fully realized the magnitude of one man's service to humanity and his colossal commitment to the ideal of freedom for all, irrespective of race, colour, creed or gender.

We all know something of what Nelson Mandela, the world's most famous former prisoner, endured and achieved, but somehow I only grasped the enormity of his inspiring life of contribution on July 18, 2008, his 90th birthday.

It took the unusual scenario of spending time in the cell of former prisoner number 46664, while being interviewed live by BBC Radio as I sat on a threadbare blanket on the floor of that miserable little room, to put things into a proper perspective. What a tribute to the human spirit that he survived 17 years in that cell to emerge as an icon of forgiveness and a worthy first president of a democratic South Africa.

On that special day I had arranged for my friends Braam Malherbe and David Grier, two extreme athletes, to run a combined 90 km around the famous prison island as part of worldwide celebrations commemorating Madiba's 90th birthday – also spotlighting our Operation Smile fundraising run around the coastline of South Africa.

Initially I was turned down by the Robben Island museum authorities when I suggested the run, and now we were broadcasting positive messages around the globe while living Braam's credo that 'Nothing is Impossible.'

"What an incredible honour," David, a 48-year-old celebrity chef, insisted: "I thought of the sweat beading on my body and imagined all the tears of pain and finally tears of joy shed on Robben Island. I'll remember this day for the rest of my life."

Braam, a 51-year-old motivational speaker and youth developer, echoed the sentiment. "I felt very humble standing in his cell and seeing how tiny it was. It was a gift to be able to imagine what he went through and to know that he came out of that horrible little hole without bitterness, but with love, forgiveness, respect and a reverence for life," Braam said.

Extreme athletes David Grier and Braam Malherbe in the tiny Robben Island cell that imprisoned Nelson Mandela for so many years

"While we were running I thought that the physical pain and stress in my body was nothing compared to what Madiba and others suffered for so long, and I thought of the challenge he issued, when he said: 'It is time for new hands to lift the burdens – it is in your hands now.'"

For a change I was involved in an event that wasn't about pure adventure, ego or personal gratification, our goal being to raise millions to fund reconstructive surgery for children with grotesque facial disfigurements like cleft palates, many of them from impoverished rural areas without access to proper medical treatment.

I was filling a predominantly behind-the-scenes role and it felt great, my ego being fed not by heroic personal deeds but contribution to the wider good.

The Operation Smile motto is 'changing lives one smile at a time' and it does that magnificently with surgeons and medical professionals selflessly giving of their talent and love to work incredibly long hours without financial remuneration. All agree that they are handsomely rewarded when they witness the transformation to the self-esteem of their young patients, many of whom have known the cruel mockery and psychological abuse of their peers.

For us Operation Smile was an astonishing adventure, my role being to help plan the runners' route each day as they ran, hiked, paddled and swam a smile around one of the most beautiful coastlines on the planet.

Each day I'd mentally tick off places I wanted to visit again, little realising then that the greatest gift was not in the scenery I visited during the 100-day endurance feat, but in my growing realisation that my own life could be far bigger and more ambitious, especially if I committed to serving the wider well-being of the Earth and its inhabitants.

If there was a pivotal day, or days, it was when we visited a rural hospital in the town of Mount Frere to offer moral support to more than 50 people with hideous facial disfigurements.

Our macho athletes had run through months of pain without protest, but their tough guy images crumbled when they came face-to-face with young children destined for life-changing facial operations. Both were moved to tears.

"Suddenly what we are doing is real and urgent," Braam said. "Meeting the children and spending time with them has been a profoundly emotional experience for us."

Little Zama with Braam before her life-changing operation

While at the hospital we received a message that a mother bound for the hospital with her disfigured daughter, wouldn't make it after all. The bus she had been travelling on throughout the night had caught fire 100 kilometres away.

"We'll fetch her," I volunteered, David immediately insisting he'd come as well.

After a hurried drive, a number of phone calls and considerable confusion, we paced tensely, wondering where they had got to.

Then suddenly we saw them and waved, five-year-old Zama racing towards us and wrapping limpet-like arms around our legs, her face radiant with joy, despite the ugly disfigurement. It was a beautiful heart-opening moment and I was touched as seldom before.

In the drive to the hospital her mum Nompumelelo Makhubo, a cleaner from the distant town of Vrede, admitted that many earlier attempts to arrange an operation had failed and Zama had stopped attending pre-school because the other children made fun of her.

During the next couple of days David and I spent many hours with both of them, also attending sessions to prepare her psychologically for the complex operation, before finally scrubbing up and donning theatre garb for what we knew would be a life-changing experience.

Normally I'm very squeamish at the sight of blood and once fainted when my dog was being stitched up, but this time I knew I owed it to Zama and the other children to be there offering moral support and praying for happy outcomes.

I spent 11 hours in surgery that day and emerged exhausted and elated.

One of the most incredible moments was when little Zama regained consciousness and was handed a mirror. Astonishment turned to wonder and delight and within hours she was showing newfound confidence as she helped other children in the ward, covering them with a blanket or offering reassurances.

Once I heard a patter of running feet and turned just as she launched herself into my arms, hugging me and grinning delightedly. Can there be a greater gift than that?

CHAPTER TWENTY TWO

INTO THE WILDS

We have to stop speaking about the Earth being in need of healing.
The Earth does not need healing. We do.
Our task is to rediscover ourselves in Nature.
It is an individual choice. And how or where do we begin?
We begin exactly where we are right now,
when we look at the world as a mirror,
when we discover that our sense of freedom and
authenticity is linked to the well-being and authenticity of others –
and that includes the animals, the trees and the land.

— *IAN McCALLUM*, AUTHOR, POET, PSYCHIATRIST AND WILDERNESS GUIDE

An eagle soaring high above the Cape's jagged Groot Winterhoek mountains might wonder what this solitary human is doing sitting naked and exposed on a rock in the sizzling heat of summer.

Friends are equally perplexed: why would I voluntarily forsake the comforts of home to spend four days and nights in the wilderness without food or proper shelter? And pay for the experience!

Have I truly lost my marbles, or is there truth in the belief that wilderness holds the key to humankind's tortured quest for inner peace, joy and a real sense of purpose?

Poets, philosophers, naturalists and even some politicians increasingly acknowledge the role of wilderness in maintaining a balance in our lives, recognising that it is to the womb of the wilds that we can return to at least briefly to escape the pressures of modern life, and re-establish a connection with the land and ourselves.

So I find myself shuffling into the dawn under the weight of a rucksack stuffed with a sleeping bag, inflatable mattress, tarpaulin and outdoor clothing for all seasons. I have plenty of water but not so much as an energy bar between me and possible starvation.

I've also left the trappings of modern civilisation behind, temporarily parting with my watch, cellphone, laptop and GPS. I'll be steered by intuition rather than technology.

Yeah, maybe I am nuts, although as the sun warms my face and I'm serenaded by birdcalls against a magnificent mountain backdrop, I'm filled with excitement and a strange elation. I've wanted to do something like this forever.

I'd fantasised about an extreme wilderness experience with the San Bushmen of the Kalahari, but instead I've signed up for an 11-day Vision Quest facilitated by two charismatic Capetonians, Judy Bekker and Valerie Morris, who insist: "The need for deep reflection time is increasingly evident in our corporate societies and our communities."

"The Vision Quest is a personal transformation process that is part of an ancient tradition with wilderness playing a significant role in the quest for a new direction in life."

The programme, which usually starts and finishes at their tranquil seaside home in Cape Town, is tailored for small groups of individuals seeking quiet time to review their lives, formulate new plans or simply ritualize a turning point like the transition from youth to adulthood, or perhaps to elderhood in the case of a person retiring or celebrating a 60th or 70th birthday.

The concept is certainly not new. History abounds with stories of inspirational leaders who withdrew from society for a period to fast alone in the wilds and seek a new vision, obvious examples being Jesus, Buddha and Mohammed.

For many the process helps deal with a career change, a health challenge, the loss of a loved one or the beginning or end of a relationship.

It is a carefully guided experience, which includes four nights solo in the wilderness, and is based on the rites of passage practised by various indigenous peoples, among them the Native Americans.

I'm not especially interested in ritual or tradition, and also wonder what I could possibly learn from two overweight, fifty-something women? How's that for a shockingly misguided first impression and hugely inappropriate judgement? While I'm leaner and fitter and have spent much of my time in the wilds, I find myself captivated by the facilitation skills and wisdom accumulated by Judy and Valerie during two decades of guiding questers of all ages and backgrounds. And soon I love them to bits and am appalled that I ever judged them!

A powerful camaraderie develops within our motley group which becomes increasingly supportive, until it is time to forsake the comforts and venture on a two-and-a-half hour drive from Cape Town to the mountains.

Each individual finds a suitable spot for a solo retreat, be it a cave or overhanging rock ledge, carrying 20 litres of water to their new 'home' before returning to the base camp where we share a last supper and evening under the stars.

Solo time begins the next morning and for some it is terrifying initially as fears are confronted. How will it feel to be truly alone and what if there's a meeting with wild creatures including snakes, spiders and scorpions? Then there's the horror of extreme boredom. What do you do when you can't switch on the TV or make a call?

We are a small group of individuals ranging from a charismatic young man in his 20s to a gentle, artistic woman in her late 60s who is mourning the loss of her lifetime lover and partner.

More than one quester is close to tears when heading out from the sanctuary of base camp to solo time. One turns back, insisting: "I can't do this," but is gently persuaded to try again.

Another quester, who is a leading businessman, surrenders one cellphone but secrets another into his backpack, only to discover there is no signal in the mountains anyway. He'll be alone with himself, perhaps for the first time ever.

My greatest fear is of squandering the time and returning from the wilderness without clarity and a clear course of action.

Each of us has been asked to write out a sacred intention, mine being: *"To find the peace and joy deep within, living a blessed life of fulfilment, abundance and unconditional love – given and received – that will help heal the planet. May my Life and writings inspire others to be more."*

I've made a pact with nature that I'll do all in my power to help undo the damage wreaked upon the environment. I'll also continue to expose others to the wonders of wilderness and all its healing properties.

I've always been at home in nature and feel welcomed back, inwardly vowing to scale the peaks of my personal potential and to help others to do the same while conquering their fears.

I follow fresh leopard spoor from a pool where it drank in the night, losing the tracks in a jumble of boulders near where I eventually find my new home.

It is a time of exhilaration, joy, discomfort and occasional hilarity. I puncture my inflatable mattress and find myself living literally between a rock and a hard place. The heavens also open on the first night and I'm soaked, not having bothered to erect a tarpaulin for shelter. Hey, nobody said Africa was for wimps!

For the first time in years time slows down to a crawl, four amazing days of wonder and adventure seeming to last forever, while the nights are endless. I celebrate the cycles of nature, my day not divided by traditional mealtimes, but the position of the sun, moon and stars.

Am I hungry? I decide that fasting is easy without the distraction of mealtimes, refrigerators and dispensing machines, although I occasionally do feel light-headed.

Funnily enough, it is the idea of going without food that is most daunting for most people. "Fasting for four days and nights does not harm the body provided there are no medical reasons why the person shouldn't fast," Judy insists. "We are overtly protective and in the many years of running Vision Quests everybody has come back alive without any serious injury."

Will I or any of my fellow questers be the first blot on an unblemished track record? I hope not.

A Quest allows plenty of time for introspection and self-analysis and I ask many questions of myself, some deep and some practical.

Am I bored without my technology and toys? No, again I feel energised, although some questers have different stories to tell, initially hating the harshness of their mountain environment.

Looking back I decide my romance with ego and materialism has been great fun – I loved being a race driver, rally driver, record breaker, 4x4 expedition guide and high-profile editor. Now, after impacting so heavily on the Earth for decades, it is payback time.

And wilderness is the womb for my rebirth.

In a sense it is a symbolic death and rebirth as you sculpt the person you choose to be and design a life that is a truer reflection of your higher self.

Self-portrait during solo time in the wilderness

Conservationist Ian Player, founder of the Wilderness Leadership School and an inspiration since I met him during my early 20s, maintains that in our wild places the ancient spirit, older than the spirit of man, still survives.

"What we have in these places," he says, "is the most precious of worldly gifts, a sense of the spiritual connection between human beings and the land. If we protect and nurture this wilderness it could be our greatest contribution to the modern world and, sensitively managed, it could provide enormous benefits to us because it is a renewable natural resource."

We all feel it powerfully during our solo retreats, although it takes time to slow down and get into sync with our new environment.

I feel I've come home. It is only in nature and especially in wilderness that I'm truly happy and consistently at peace. Here I can quiet all those irrelevant thoughts – the mind Buddhists call 'the chattering monkey' – to achieve a measure of clarity.

Sitting on my rock I become aware of fresh perspectives. The big things that troubled me in the outside world seem insignificant and I'm enthralled by the little creatures that are my companions, excitedly observing a cycle of life from tadpole to frog in one small rock pool.

I think I'm losing my fear of dying although I'm definitely not ready to go. Life is too delicious and too much fun to be relinquished just yet. I recognize that I'm a tri-part being and try to differentiate between what body, mind and soul are wanting and wishing to be.

Four amazing days and nights seem to last forever and with each passing hour there is growing calm and contentment, although on the last night I engage in an all-night vigil where I confront my demons, laying them to rest before the sun rises on a new day and a new life.

Some issues have bubbled up unexpectedly from the depths … anger directed at my father; sadness that I wasn't a more loving son, brother and husband, although I give myself a much higher score for my performance as a Dad.

Day Five dawns with a beauty so intense I could weep tears of joy and gratitude. Almost reluctantly I pack up, dress for the first time in days and head towards base camp where I'm met by hugs, rumpled hairdos, stubbled chins and tanned faces radiating confidence and fresh purpose.

The sense of love and camaraderie is pervasive and the storytelling begins amid laughter and tears. All agree that the Vision Quest process has been profound.

Maybe I am a slow learner? I repeat the Quest ritual three times in the space of two years, embarking upon nature-based journeys into the wilderness of my own soul. And yet, although there are some spectacular insights, I'm not done. I continue to yearn for wildness and deeper explorations of the untamed territory of the soul.

Life is so exciting … and two lovely ladies have taught me so much about being one with the wilds – and also about the folly of making snap judgements: or any judgements for that matter. Judy and Valerie are precious gifts and prized friends.

HONOURING SACRED INTENTIONS

The weeks and months following my first quest are remarkable – a flurry of emails and a reunion dinner reveal that each and every participant has undergone profound changes, slaying many a dragon and boldly venturing forth into the new world.

Although I've always been passionate about nature I've never felt this level of connectedness before, enjoying a number of exciting encounters.

Every day for the first fortnight I am blessed with superb sightings of eagles in the immediate vicinity of where I live in Cape Town, a black eagle circling above my home and another swooping in front of me while hiking Chapman's Peak Pass.

Once, while lying on a rock ledge in the sun, lizards crawl over me and sit on my body, unconcerned. On another outing into nature a deadly boomslang snake circles back towards me several times, coming up close but showing no hint of malice.

This chimp has known the worst and best of human behaviour

At Chimp Eden in Mpumalanga, which has featured extensively on *Animal Planet*, I look deep in the soulful eyes of a rescued chimp that has known the cruellest of human behaviour and feel such intense sadness and compassion, somehow understanding the animal's pain. How can we humans treat another being so unkindly?

And, on hikes on the Table Mountain chain, I've twice had a troop of baboons approach me and my friend Antoinette, the little ones scampering up and playfully undoing shoelaces, gentling squeezing fingers or softly tugging at our hair and clothing.

When the huge alpha male initially approaches I feel a surge of fear until I realize there is only curiosity and an expression devoid of hostility. For more than a minute it gazes intently into our eyes from just centimetres away, seeming to decide we are OK. The troop then sits and moves around us on 'our' rock for several minutes before setting off in search of tasty roots and other morsels.

A few days later they again seem to seek us out, the dominant animal sunbathing on his back nearby while others play around us. I don't want to disturb the moment, but eventually snap cellphone pictures of four youngsters engaging with Antoinette, one meticulously checking her hair with gently probing fingers.

"I've never felt so blessed," she insists. "It seems that they recognise us and are totally accepting, realising we wish them no harm. If only we humans can do the same for them."

CHAPTER TWENTY THREE

THE MAGIC OF FINDHORN

*The essence of this community is to bring heaven
down to Earth, to learn to do everything with love.*
— *EILEEN CADDY,* FINDHORN COMMUNITY CO-FOUNDER

Increasingly I've come to delight in the invisible forces of the Universe that draw you towards your destiny like a giant magnet, edging you nearer to the people, places and events that you need to experience along your life path.

Have you ever noticed how something will keep appearing in your awareness, whether it is in the newspaper you are reading, the movie you've just watched, the words of a song or even the conversation of a stranger? And so it was with Findhorn. More than once I'd heard mention of this unusual community on the other side of the world, although initially that wasn't enough to grab my attention.

Funnily enough it was pivotal to the spiritual growth of a great friend and former lover, awakening her to the presence of unseen beings and worlds, and that purely from reading about the pioneering community in northern Scotland. She'd never been there and still hasn't, but talks fondly and knowingly of Findhorn as a place of magic and miracles. To some she might seem a bit airy-fairy although I have come to totally respect her wisdom.

Clearly I needed a bigger nudge and finally got it when another friend unexpectedly handed me a book, insisting: "Here's something you might find interesting." It looked like the kind of 1970s book you'd find in a second-hand junk market and definitely not something I'd normally pick up. It was called *The Magic of Findhorn* and the blurb could have sent me sprinting in the opposite direction:

'The full, fascinating true story of a miraculous community where a modern Garden of Eden grows, where people are reborn, and faith, love and energy triumph ... AN EYEWITNESS ACCOUNT BY PAUL HAWKEN.'

Had somebody overdosed on mushrooms or marijuana, I wondered? Flipping to the back cover of the book I noted that the Findhorn gardeners grew 40-pound cabbages and roses that bloomed in the snow. What is the source of this spectacular success, the book inquired? Did I care? I'm a petrolhead and not a gardener.

**John Willoner, Dorothy Maclean and Jonathan Caddy where it
all began at Findhorn's original caravan**

And yet my interest was aroused by the author's observation: "Findhorn may be a manifestation of light and power which could transform our planet within a lifetime." I started reading …

Clearly Hawken was something of a sceptic to begin with, although time spent with the fledgling community would change that as he came to know the power of the place. Something was happening here, something extraordinary that visiting experts described as a mysterious Factor X.

The origins of the now famous community couldn't have been more inauspicious, former RAF squadron leader Peter Caddy and his wife Eileen, their three young boys and friend Dorothy Maclean arriving with a caravan in tow after he'd lost his job as a hotel manager. That was on November 17, 1962 and the three adults imagined they'd be at the Findhorn Bay Caravan Park for a few days at most.

It was a bleak and inhospitable place consisting of sand dunes and prickly gorse bushes and in winter it was wearing its least welcoming face, Findhorn being further north than Moscow and parts of Alaska.

Strangely, despite a superb track record which included catering for up to a million men daily during the war, Peter failed to find work and the six of them lived on a pittance in the caravan as the weeks stretched into months. They had to do something to survive and began a vegetable garden.

Each of the trio had individually spent years tuning in to their inner guidance and each knew their calling was to be together, although they had no idea that they would form the nucleus of what would grow into a world-renowned spiritual community, holistic education centre and celebrated ecovillage.

Dorothy was later to tell me: "Looking around now I am absolutely amazed and can hardly believe it. I think of the three ordinary people that we were, but we had the commitment to God and that takes you everywhere. One person with God is in the majority."

Eileen meditated for many hours each night, listening to the small, still voice within and Peter, the action man, followed that guidance in complete trust.

Soon Dorothy's remarkable role became apparent when she tuned into the overlighting intelligence of the nature kingdom and received very specific and practical instructions about what to grow and how and when to do it. Despite poor sandy soil in what had been little more than a rubbish dump in the dunes, the miracle of Findhorn's gardens began to unfold.

It is a story of unwavering faith that moved me deeply, although when I first visited the Findhorn Foundation website I was fascinated more by what had manifested decades later, the ecovillage boasting the lowest recorded ecological footprint in the developed world. I had to get there and see what I could learn about living simply and sustainably in harmony with the Earth.

My opportunity arose when a month-long ecovillage training course was advertised, beginning early in 2009. It came at an awkward time as my finances were disastrous, although I sent off a deposit to secure my place anyway. Then I realized I couldn't possibly afford to go and tried to stop the payment. There was a mix-up and the bookings office deducted the full amount via my credit card, plunging me into panic.

In the midst of frantically trying to reverse the transaction a great calm came over me and it was suddenly clear: I had to go. I'd sort out my precarious finances when I returned home.

And what a gift that month proved to be, changing my life forever. The intense programme kept us busy long into the nights as we immersed ourselves in permaculture principles, working in local organic vegetable gardens and visiting eco homes. Some houses known as eco-mobiles were built on a caravan chassis while others had been fashioned from whisky barrels, taking recycling to the logical extreme in an area famed for the precious amber liquid.

Sun and wind energy were harnessed with four whirling wind turbines supplying electricity needs and producing enough to sell around 30 percent of the surplus back to the national energy grid, while The Living Machine used an entirely chemical-free process of plants, organisms and bacteria to convert sewage into clear water. I was bewitched by all this modern-day magic!

I'd glimpsed another way of living and became very excited about the idea of creating a mini-Findhorn back in South Africa, even using Google Earth to locate an ideal property near Cape Point, half an hour from home.

More important than what I was learning about ecovillage principles was what was happening to our group of 30 individuals of all ages, from all walks of life around the globe.

I feel sheepish when I think back to that first day as we stood in a circle holding hands. Being a macho South African I didn't like this one bit and said so: "I'm not comfortable standing around holding hands," I announced, "and especially not with guys." The group facilitators never said a word and smiled knowingly. Within days my heart had opened wide and I was in love with each of the group and all of life, dropping the barriers I had built up around me and happily holding hands with whomever.

I no longer saw being the strong silent type as a virtue, finally appreciating the value and honesty of open-hearted sharing with those around me. It was a safe space and a place of healing and wonderful insights and since then I've seen it happen again and again to participants in Experience Week. It is a beautiful thing and part of what attracts thousands of visitors each year.

While Findhorn seems idyllic to outsiders and short-term visitors it has been likened to a pressure cooker, a laboratory for change and a spiritual hothouse. Inner growth is intensified and accelerated and the process can be painful, often leading to stress, loneliness, illness and sometimes burnout. Hey, whoever suggested the evolution of the soul would be easy.

These days Findhorn is also an international centre of learning that is linked to a number of universities and is known as the Findhorn Foundation, so as not to be confused with the adjoining village of Findhorn where the more conservative citizens initially regarded their neighbours suspiciously as hippies.

Coming from South Africa I marvelled at the sense of safety in a crime-free environment and in a month I never heard a voice raised in anger nor had my sleep punctuated by an alarm. In fact, I slowed life down, walking everywhere and never once driving a car. And me a former race and rally driver!

Often I was surprised by the high-powered credentials of individuals choosing to do menial work, with all staff members earning the same incredibly meagre wage.

Some, like Craig Gibsone, have been here almost from the beginning. He is a charismatic 70-year-old Australian with a mischievous grin who has the vitality of a much younger man, delighting in extracting the best from the shyest members of the group in his role as a 'focaliser'. That's Findhorn-speak for facilitator!

He arrived in 1969 and never really left: "I sensed and felt Findhorn as an experimental field of energy – a laboratory where humans could work on other levels of themselves. Findhorn has been very good at developing the fullness of the psyche of the human soul."

He tells me that an important factor has been the continuous evolution of the community, the collective embracing young and old, differing philosophies, and people from all walks of life and all nationalities.

The glue, it seems, is a freedom from dogma or boundaries, community members attempting always to respect and accommodate each other, and to work in co-operation with Nature.

There's a wonderful sense of well-being and joy that bubbles up at the most unexpected moments. People smile and laugh a lot, as well as having the courage to confront all the difficult questions. Who are we? Where are we going? Is there a way out of the mess Spaceship Earth finds itself in at the beginning of the 21st century? Can we build a new social paradigm where money and economic growth are not the primary motivators?

Here people are encouraged to always question, knowing that it is at the edge of our comfort zone that life begins.

I am deeply moved when the youngest member of our group, 21-year-old Elizabeth Brocke demands tearfully: "Why can't I simply have fun like other young people my age, instead of facing up to all the realities that growing up at Findhorn has made me so painfully aware of? It isn't fair!"

Days later I join her and two other young adults in a spontaneous moment of exuberance. We leap naked into a loch against the stunningly beautiful backdrop of forests blanketed in snow – the water is covered in ice in places and we laugh like children, feeling incredibly, gratefully alive.

Two of my best days are spent with the Trees for Life project aimed at restoring the Caledonian Forest, but a heavy snowfall means that instead of planting young trees, we collect seeds from the indigenous Scots pines that are so threatened, only 1% of the original forests remaining.

The passion and unwavering commitment of project founder Alan Watson Featherstone is an inspirational call to arms.

So what's Findhorn really like?

My first impression is of spotless cleanliness despite a shortage of funds – if you are doing God's work, nothing less than perfection will do.

I stay in a refurbished mobile home that is very comfy, five of us each having our own bedroom and sharing a communal lounge, dining room, kitchen and bathroom. It is typical of accommodation many share, with a progressive move away from old-fashioned caravans that are inefficient, expensive to heat and often made of toxic materials.

Lunches and dinners are taken in the Community Centre and are always animated, little groups often adjourning to one of the mobile homes or the village green for more fun and laughter, or maybe a game of volleyball.

A tradition is that work is love in action and once a week we all do KP (which stands for kitchen patrol), and one afternoon a week I join the park maintenance team, helping build a wooden ramp to the Universal Hall, gutting a bathroom and performing minor and mostly unfamiliar handyman tasks. It is fun and empowering and I like the motto: "If it isn't fun, it isn't sustainable!"

I begin to understand why I was so powerfully drawn to visit the chilly north: it is so much more than a curiosity about connecting to ancestral roots, both my parents originally hailing from Scotland.

Today, half a century after Peter, Eileen and Dorothy first arrived, their legacy is global and their messages of love and sharing are timeless. We must help to raise consciousness and be the change we wish to see in the world.

Just before my month is up most of us take part in a Sweat Lodge and construct a Native American-style tepee out of poles, branches and blankets, with access through a small flap. A huge fire is built outside to heat boulders until they are red hot, which are passed inside with a spade.

We sit in a circle in the darkness on the raw earth, wearing towels, and feel the heat building progressively. We have prepared our sacred intentions and each in turn speaks them to the circle.

It is a profound and moving ritual, although for me, a claustrophobic and former asthmatic, the heat and close confines become increasingly suffocating until I have to get out, crawling frantically for the exit and continuing on hands and knees towards the forest. My rising panic and dizziness is replaced by an outer body experience as I find myself looking down on the scene. I have lost my towel and I'm naked, muddy and look quite silly. I'm amused at my predicament and realize I've shed much of my attachment to ego. How I look is unimportant, which is an incredible gift in itself.

The others emerge from the sweat a few minutes later, some cooling themselves with hoses or buckets of water. I see one incredibly beautiful woman standing

A once bleak dunescape has been transformed into Findhorn's Garden of Eden

proud and erect and I'm puzzled: I know everybody in the group but don't recognise her.

Then it dawns on me that this is the same young lass who always seemed so mousy and apologetic. Now she is transformed; radiant and confident. I say to her: "You're not the person I met a month ago."

She smiles gratefully: "I feel it too and I'm glad you've noticed."

Findhorn has worked its magic, but Africa still calls me…

CHAPTER TWENTY FOUR

CRY FREEDOM!

If there are dreams about a beautiful South Africa,
there are also roads that lead to that goal.
Two of these roads could be named Goodness and Forgiveness.

— *NELSON MANDELA,* FORMER SOUTH AFRICAN PRESIDENT
AND ROBBEN ISLAND PRISONER

It came as a mild shock to realize that three decades had passed since the horror of June 1976 when I had made almost daily visits to Soweto – only returning twice in later years; once for a football final and again for a Jimmy Cliff reggae concert.

A couple of months earlier I had missed out on reggae king Bob Marley's Zimbabwe Independence Day Concert in Harare and I wasn't going to make that mistake again, heading for the musical happening in Soweto with a journalist friend.

It was a tribute to the unifying power of music as black and white came together to join Jimmy Cliff in pouring heart and soul into such numbers as *'No Woman, No Cry.'* What a beautiful day it was but surprisingly I didn't go back to Soweto again for a decade and half, perhaps avoiding too many painful memories of a nation's torment. Like so many other whites I also perceived the townships to be dangerous, especially for palefaces like myself.

Finally I felt it time. I needed to let go of the old and get to grips with the soul of democratic South Africa. That meant rewinding to June 1976 and revisiting the cataclysmic events that ultimately emancipated and united all South Africans in a common destiny.

I enlisted the help of activist-turned-tour guide Joe Motshogi who introduced me to the idea of a struggle pilgrimage, driving me from the leafy suburbs of upper-class Sandton to the vibrancy and squalor of Soweto, Johannesburg's younger and less affluent sibling. And far from being simply a serious history lesson, it turned out to be a celebration that was often characterized by fun and merriment, Joe smiling and laughing a lot as he enthusiastically greeted locals wherever we went. Tune in to the heartbeat of the country's largest and most famous black township and you marvel at the power of the human spirit to forgive.

I met ordinary people who inspired me with their wonderful attitudes and warm welcome, despite often tortured pasts.

The Hector Pieterson memorial honours all the young heroes and heroines who gave their lives in the struggle for freedom, and especially Hector, the 13-year-old gunned down during the protest against the enforced use of Afrikaans as a language of teaching in black schools. Back then Afrikaans was seen as the language of the *apartheid* oppressors.

Inevitably I came face to face with that famous photograph again, feeling the pain of those awful moments when a dying Hector Pieterson was carried by a stranger while his older sister Antoinette ran alongside, screaming. But I hadn't expected to meet with her, now Mrs Antoinette Sithole, a respected member of the community and a 50-something mum working at the museum.

I felt awkward asking her about that dreadful day that changed so many lives forever, but Joe said it was fine, urging me to go ahead. I even snapped her photograph alongside the haunting life-sized black and white original.

"I can forgive the people who did this, but I can't forget." she told me tearfully. "I used to have a lot of anger and eventually realized I couldn't live like this. I decided to take the picture and pretend that I was an outsider and not part of it. That paved the way to be not overly emotional."

Now, she says: "We must mix all God's colours, including black and white, like flowers, to create something quite beautiful."

I feel that is happening and have so many remarkable memories of my all-day tour with Joe.

An ideal starting point, and the one we chose, was Liliesleaf Farm in the exclusive suburb of Rivonia where a police raid in 1963 dealt a major blow to the leadership of the African National Council and the struggle for liberation.

Nelson Mandela, wearing blue workman's overalls and posing as a servant named David Motsamayi, was arrested along with 11 others, the now famous Rivonia Treason Trialists including Govan Mbeki, father of former South African president Thabo Mbeki.

Interestingly, half of the 12 accused were not black Africans, reminding us that many from all walks fought to create the democratic Rainbow Nation we celebrate today. It would be good if racist elements within the ruling ANC leadership remembered and honoured that idealism and the sacrifices of South Africans of all colours.

At the opening of the trial, lawyer Mandela chose to conduct his own defence and made one of his most famous and impassioned speeches: "During my lifetime, I have dedicated myself to this struggle of the African people. I have fought against white domination and I have fought against black domination. I have cherished the ideal of a democratic and free society in which all persons live together in harmony and with equal opportunities.

"It is an ideal which I hope to live for and to achieve. But if needs be, it is an ideal for which I'm prepared to die."

The accused had expected the death sentence, laughing with relief and disbelief when life sentences were handed down at the end of the courtroom drama.

Another major attraction which should be on every Freedom Tour itinerary is the Apartheid Museum, which has been built in a style reminiscent of a prison, faithfully re-creating the dark, brooding mood of life under a repressive regime.

And yet, each time I visit, I find myself uplifted and inspired by the human spirit's ability to soar above adversity and seemingly impossible challenges.

I'm fascinated too by the reactions of so many young visitors, running the gamut of emotions from shock, horror and revulsion to pride and joy at the road post-democratic South Africa has taken.

These places are a journey rather than a destination – lest we forget!

———— ✥ ————

Like a boomerang I like to return to the symbol of hope that is Soweto, recently enlisting the help of Inga to tailor my own self-drive itinerary ending in Vilakazi Street, the local equivalent of Hollywood Boulevard where you might easily spot celebrity stars of the freedom struggle.

Vilakazi residents proudly claim that their street is the only one in the world that has been home to two Nobel laureates, Nelson Mandela and Archbishop Emeritus Desmond Tutu, the former Archbishop of Cape Town who headed the Truth and Reconciliation Commission.

But mostly the street is about having a good time and we soon find ourselves in animated conversation with locals and a sprinkling of enthusiastic international visitors at Sakhumzi Restaurant.

Earlier we'd hung out with newfound friends at The Shack, a township pub known as a shebeen, where the beer of choice was chilled Namibian lager drunk straight from large bottles, a group of women gyrating to loud music while the menfolk played a game of pool, amid much good-natured merriment.

There's a great warmth and sense of community that's missing in many cities where neighbours don't know each other and live behind high security walls.

Of course, no visit to Vilakazi Street is complete without a tour of the modest 'matchbox' home that Mandela shared with his former wife Winnie, the original facebrick house now dwarfed by a huge museum façade.

I also mixed in the fun of a bicycle tour run from Lebo's Soweto Backpackers, which ranges from two hours to a full day. Our half-day excursion involved gentle pedalling with lots of stops to visit tourism sites and meet with locals in an informal atmosphere.

Expect to see the obvious major attractions as well sipping traditional beer in a shebeen, munching popular local dishes and being warmly welcomed everywhere, the children often running alongside and whooping with delight, or exchanging exuberant 'high-five' hand slaps.

Inevitably poverty is widely evident, but there was no begging and it was safe to prop our bicycles up against a wall and wander off on walking excursions. We always felt entirely secure and Sowetans seemed pleased that we were taking the trouble to better understand the sprawling township and its inhabitants.

If you don't feel like the exercise then a visit to the Backpackers will be an eye-opener anyway, showing what can be done with imagination, creativity and boundless energy.

Lebo Malepa, a young Sowetan with a vision, has transformed his grandparent's home into an 18-bed backpackers' lodge with a stunning outside entertainment area framed by reeds and palm fronds, mixing reggae and township music. Africa meets Jamaica!

Curiously, comparatively few South Africans, and even fewer pale-skinned Africans are among Lebo's usual clientele and are missing out on fun-filled insights. My invitation is to get with the spirit of Ubuntu*, meet the people and celebrate South Africa's miraculous transformation. What a journey it has been!

---

* Ubuntu is the essence of being human and refers to an African tradition of community and welcoming strangers. It recognises that we can't exist in isolation and celebrates interconnectedness with all of humanity.

CHAPTER TWENTY FIVE

EPIPHANY

Why do we have to listen to our hearts?
Because, wherever your heart is,
that is where you'll find your treasure.
— *PAULO COELHO,* NOVELIST

The idea of a really big walk had been looming for years and yet I never saw it as part of my life purpose, suspecting rather that it would be a great adventure and personal feat of endurance.

I knew I'd undertake an epic trek someday and a favourite idea was - and is - to walk from the foot of Africa to its summit, starting at Cape Agulhas, the southernmost tip and finishing on Kilimanjaro's melting icecap. And I figured I might as well make it a celebration of mountain magic and bag all of Africa's Big Five, scaling the next four highest peaks as part of the same continuous hike.

While entertaining this dream I simultaneously searched for meaning and suspect that former world boxing champ and social activist Muhammad Ali was right when he said: "Service to others is the rent you pay for your room here on Earth."

My path to service during 2010 found me in Findhorn, working as an unpaid volunteer in the community's Communications office and beginning each day with a meditation in the Sanctuary. As well as trying to send love and light to a troubled world, I focussed on my great friend Anna Breytenbach, my visualisation seeing her conquer cancer and return to vibrant good health. I also added a daily prayer: "Please guide and inspire me and show me how I might best be of service."

Answers weren't immediate, although I had faith they'd come.

Findhorn is an incredible gift and there seems to be amazing synchronicity here. It was during my first visit the previous year that I'd picked up a book entitled *No Destination* by Satish Kumar, the spiritual and ecological activist who is editor of *Resurgence* magazine and narrator of BBC2's *Earth Pilgrim* programme.

Never before had I encountered another's philosophy that resonated so closely with what I'd instinctively felt from early childhood, his subsequent *Earth Pilgrim* book echoing my own thoughts.

He became a pilgrim at the age of four when he walked with his mother to the farm, she insisting that walking there was a pilgrimage, whereas if they

Resurgence editor Satish Kumar is a major source of inspiration

travelled on horseback or in a camel cart, then they were just interested in getting there.

"My mother would say that when you touch the Earth, you are touching sacred space – a divine space – and God is present in the Earth. And everything upon this Earth is a manifestation of the divine spirit in physical form. You have to imagine that this flower you are looking at is not just a physical flower; it is an embodiment of divine spirit. The flower is an intelligent and animate being."

Imagine my excitement when I discovered Satish was visiting Findhorn to address the Inspired Action conference, never suspecting I'd have dinner and lunch with him in the Community Centre on successive days.

"Transformation is a way of life," he says, using the birth of the Findhorn Community as a vivid illustration of how it was born out of the actions of three people who set up home in a caravan half a century earlier.

His own transformation was no less dramatic - also beginning in 1962 - when he and a friend were sipping coffee in a Bangalore café and read that elderly philosopher and Nobel laureate Bertrand Russell had been arrested in an anti-nuclear demonstration in London.

"Here is a man of 90 committing civil disobedience and going to jail. What are we doing?" the two young Indian men asked themselves.

What followed was a remarkable feat of courage, endurance and faith as they undertook a 13,000 km peace pilgrimage from New Delhi through deserts, mountains, storms and snow to Moscow, Paris, London and Washington – and did so without money or provisions on the recommendation of their guru. I was enchanted by Satish; everything he said making so much sense.

Inevitably the themes of simplicity, humility, healthy relationships and sustainability are interwoven in his teachings: "Modern lifestyle is destroying the fundamentals of relationships. The consequence of a materialistic, acquisitive, fashionable, consumerist lifestyle is gross unhappiness. And that gross unhappiness is the price we are paying on a personal level."

We are also paying a high price on the social level with the injustice of fabulous wealth alongside dreadful slums and shanty towns in many cities.

"Then there are the environmental consequences," Satish cautions. "Everything we are producing and consuming is based on one source of energy: oil, which we consume at the rate of millions of barrels each day. One consequence is global warming and another is global wars. So a fundamental change in our collective way of life is a personal, social and environmental imperative.

"These systems on which modern life is based were built by humans, and can be changed by humans. If our systems are damaging personal, social and environmental coherence, then we need to redesign them and such redesigning requires a new ecological and spiritual consciousness.

"When people see this and make the connection between their own lifestyle and the negative consequences that result when it is reproduced on a global scale, then I think they will welcome a redesigning of the world and a lifestyle which is elegant, simple, comfortable, beautiful, joyful and happy. If we can do this we will not need three or four or more planets and can live happily on our one planet.

"We talk of human rights but we need to recognize the rights of nature."

Just a few weeks later Satish is back, this time to share the theme of *A Journey through Inner and Outer Landscapes* during a five-day workshop co-hosted by Daniel Wahl of the Findhorn College. I'm desperate to attend but lack the funds to sign up when Communications focaliser Eva Ward steps in: "You must do it. We'll find the money somewhere."

The programme includes walks with Satish through the Findhorn Dunes, along the beach at Culbin Sands and through the ancient woods at Cawdor Castle, where I have a powerful feeling of religious awe such as I've only rarely known when entering a great cathedral, temple or mosque. Nature is my place of worship.

Often we walk in total silence as we explore inner and outer landscapes, even deliberately experiencing our beautiful Findhorn environment with eyes closed,

Peace Pilgrim walked with her message for 28 years

while being guided through an exercise in trust that amplifies the images we receive through the other senses.

There are so many lightbulb moments it is the spiritual equivalent of a discotheque with one of those rotating mirrored balls reflecting light everywhere.

As Satish and I talk the nucleus of an idea takes shape in my mind. I imagine a pilgrimage in 2012 to celebrate the community's 50th birthday, not realising I'm perhaps visualising a blueprint for my own journey.

"Either we can act as tourists and look at the Earth as a source of goods and services for our personal use, or we can become Earth Pilgrims and treat the planet with reverence and gratitude," Satish says. "Tourists value the Earth and all her natural riches only in terms of their usefulness to themselves, while pilgrims perceive the planet as sacred and recognize the intrinsic value of all life."

Already 73, he insists that life is to be lived in every moment. "As a pilgrim I discover the mystery, the magic, the meaning and the magnificence of life in every step I take, in every sound I hear and in every sight I see."

He adds: "Great things can happen with small actions," quoting the example of African American activist Rosa Parks who became known as the mother of the modern civil rights movement after she had refused to give up her seat on a bus to a white passenger in 1955.

Her actions inspired Martin Luther King Jr who may not have lived to see his dreams become reality, but just over 40 years after his death President Barack Obama is installed in the White House.

In conversation Satish casually mentions a woman called Peace Pilgrim who walked tirelessly for 28 years throughout North America with a message of peace. A couple of nights later I decide to visit the Boutique, a shed at Findhorn where cast-off clothing and books are left for those that need it. The lighting is gloomy but a small blue book jumps out at me. It's called *Peace Pilgrim: Her Life and Work in her Own Words*. Wow, talk about synchronicity.

I start reading immediately and keep going deep into the night, finishing the book and then starting again. Known simply as Peace Pilgrim, she was a remarkable silver-haired woman who vowed to: "Remain a wanderer until mankind has learned the way of peace, walking until given shelter and fasting until given food."

A pilgrim's job, she said, was to rouse people from apathy and to make them think, adding: "Love is the greatest power on Earth. It conquers all things."

Penniless and walking her talk without any organisational backing, she touched the hearts and lives of countless thousands who were inspired by her message of achieving peace between nations, individuals and that all important inner peace that is the vital starting point.

Born Mildred Lizette Norman in 1908, she went on to become a major force for good whose life as a peace activist, pacifist and vegetarian personified faith, commitment and simplicity; her only possessions being those she carried in the pockets sewn into her tunic.

"Unnecessary possessions are unnecessary burdens," she said. "If you have them, you have to take care of them. There is great freedom in simplicity of living."

She advocated a life of service dedicated to humanity and all God's creations, delivering her message with a characteristic warmth and cheerfulness.

On July 7, 1981 she died instantly in a car accident while being driven to a talk. She was 72 and had described death as "a beautiful liberation into a freer life."

I feel that all my prayers have been answered. There are so many positive happenings in the world; my friend Anna is not only healing but has agreed to host an interspecies communications workshop at Findhorn; and I now know my path to service. I'm going to shed all unnecessary possessions and walk the equivalent of the circumference of the Earth with a message about living simply and sustainably. I'll create a website and write a book.

And I decide that I'll start walking from the sacred Isle of Iona on July 7, 2011, honouring Peace Pilgrim who passed from this life exactly 30 years earlier. "Life is like a mirror," she said. "Smile at it and it smiles back at you."

CHAPTER TWENTY SIX

FINDHORN GARDEN OF EDEN

You wonder that the spirit of a flower can speak so deeply.
Wonder not; are we not all from the One Source,
and would that Source deny life and intelligence to anything?
All of life pulsates with Life, with God.

— *DOROTHY MACLEAN,* FINDHORN COMMUNITY CO-FOUNDER

If you wish to totally immerse yourself in community life there's no better way than serving as a volunteer in the Communications office, which is an epicentre of everything happening at Findhorn.

I reasoned that I could be of service fulfilling a much-needed role as a photojournalist while simultaneously getting to know all the movers and shakers in the community. And that's exactly what happened when I joined the energetic team led by American Eva Ward, having way more fun than I expected while covering very local stories.

Imagine my astonishment when, after a few weeks, I asked Eva if she was happy with what l was doing? "You are an answer to our prayers and a gift from God," she insisted, leaving me speechless. I guess that's the difference between the dog-eat-dog corporate world and life in a spiritual community that prides itself on doing things differently in the quest to be kinder and more loving.

A central theme is nurturing and developing the full potential of each individual, whatever their role. It sounds cheesy but it's all about caring and sharing and creating a better world.

The legacy of each of the founders is evident every day in the functioning of each department. Peter Caddy believed that work is "love in action" so all tasks are tackled joyfully as a path to service, while his wife Eileen demonstrated the power of meditation and accessing that small, still voice within before making any important decisions. Dorothy Maclean, meanwhile, helped shape Findhorn's uniqueness as a community by collaborating closely with the natural world to manifest abundance and diversity in what was formerly a bleak dunescape.

So the working day begins with an attunement, in a circle holding hands, with the role of unseen beings and the overlighting intelligence of the natural world

**Dorothy Maclean is in her nineties and the sole
surviving co-founder**

invariably acknowledged. Co-creation with nature is part of the ethos and nobody
doubts its effectiveness.

A big part of my day was invariably taken up with writing for the Findhorn
website, although I delighted in contributing to the internal weekly Rainbow
Bridge magazine and publications like local newspaper the *Forres Gazette*, which I
saw as an important bridge to the wider community.

Especially fascinating was the pioneering exercise in good neighbourliness between a team from the Findhorn Foundation and senior officers of RAF Kinloss,
our immediate neighbours.

For decades the aircraft have been a source of noise, pollution and intense
irritation, especially during manoeuvres in the middle of the night, and yet our
meeting provided unexpected gifts. It revealed some common ground – and opportunities to explore closer contacts.

We were treated to an in-depth briefing by the station commander as well as a tour of the air base – nicknamed the 'Home of the Mighty Hunter' in a reference to the legendary Nimrod search and reconnaissance aircraft that enjoyed more than 40 years of faithful service.

My Dad was an RAF pilot and the visit brought out the little boy in me, along with some sympathy for the role of the military.

"We are trying to remove some of the myths and rumours about us," the commander explained, emphasising: "We do not live in a peaceful world, but we are not warmongers." On the contrary, he believed we shared the objective of world peace. "Our goal is providing for a safe and secure environment, which is the same, I believe, as striving for world peace. It might seem to some as an unachievable aim, but I'm a firm advocate of shooting for the stars with a realistic prospect of landing on the moon."

It would have been easy to demonize our military neighbours, particularly because of the shattering noise and lung-searing pollution of the aircraft. Once while walking the beach near the air base the fumes were so pervasive that I came close to gagging.

Instead of the enemy I met friendly, professional people doing the best they can, while the young engineers reminded me of our own young people with their love of cutting-edge technology, be it the latest avionics or mobile phones.

Having worked most of my life as a journalist, I decided that I needed to experience one of the traditional departments and it was agreed I'd spend time in Park Garden, my focaliser being Rona Ribeiro, a beautiful long-haired Brazilian in her mid-thirties.

"It's not just about beautifying the gardens or harvesting, but about nurturing you as well," she explained.

Instead of seeing life through a computer screen or a camera viewfinder, I found myself getting my fingers dirty and really connecting with the Earth. It felt very good, although I never suspected how pivotal it would be to my understanding of Findhorn.

My first major assignment was to help build a pond, with water flowing down three levels in a series of spirals. I'd never done anything remotely like this and nor had my lovely lady accomplices, German Maren Koopman and young Australian Nathalie Rule. When Nathalie and I expressed concerns about our inexperience we were urged to attune, seeking inner guidance and the help of the higher intelligence of the Nature kingdoms.

And we did, somewhat sheepishly in my case. It's hard to quantify or describe, except to say everything flowed so astonishingly smoothly, whether it was finding

My communications office playmates Chris, Lisa, Avalon, Yasko, Christine and Eva Ward

exactly the right-shaped rocks with which to build the pond, or positioning the pond so we didn't have to cut major tree roots. We had fun, laughed a lot and had the immense satisfaction of beautifying the original garden alongside the famous caravan where it all started.

Later I saw another face to Findhorn with the uproar when a mature tree was chopped down to try and accommodate a flatbed truck delivering our new bio-mass boiler. The path was still blocked and it became apparent that other trees would have to go or an alternate solution found.

The verdict was that the loss of the tree had been a spontaneous and ill-judged action which did not honour the tradition of inner attunement. "Our gardens and community are a place of experimentation and we do make mistakes," one elder confided. "It is important that we recognize the mistakes, forgive them and learn from them."

Ultimately two huge cranes were hired at considerable expense and the remaining trees spared. Lesson learned.

I was deeply touched that the community cared enough to dip into its modest funds to save a handful of trees.

More recently I was to gain further insights when I was tasked with trimming an unruly beech hedge that extended for 200 metres and soared more than three metres high. My first reaction was astonishment that I'd be trimming the monster hedge with a small pair of hand cutters. I imagined I'd be at it for a week or more, when I could do the job in hours with an electric or petrol-powered machine. My first thought was: "This is crazy and a huge waste of time."

Working alongside me was former German forester Kajedo Wanderer, who was snipping carefully and lovingly to ensure that no single stem or leaf was damaged unnecessarily. Wherever possible the snip was done behind foliage, so that it wasn't obvious that a stem had been severed. It was like watching a surgeon at work, although this operation was simple and routine.

Kajedo became a professional forester at 17 and has been a Findhorn gardener for three decades, latterly serving as the custodian of the trees. "It was in the company of trees that I felt closest to the Great Mystery of Life … to God," he recalled.

"The garden and the community is a microcosm of the larger world where we experience the same situations and challenges found in most places on the planet.

"How we interact with the land and soil always has a ritual aspect where we are trying to invoke kinder and more sensitive and more attuned ways of working with the Earth. When we have to trim 200 metres of beech hedge in the summer we do what needs doing in the kindest way possible and in a way that allows us to be in touch with the living plants as much as possible.

"Using a machine would cut through masses of green leaves and make them look as brown and unwell as the planet probably feels. So we have a tradition of doing it by hand with secateurs and loppers to create as little harm as possible, bearing in mind that we are working with tree beings. We are consciously trying to counterbalance the way that trees and forests are cruelly slaughtered in many places such as the Amazon.

"While it could be seen as slow and ineffectual, our role here is also to help people connect with the life-force of the plants and to raise awareness of the divinity of the natural world. With that in mind pruning a long hedge with secateurs might be the most effective way."

After overcoming my initial resistance and usual urge to do everything as quickly as possible, I settled into a gentle rhythm that I found immensely peaceful and deeply satisfying, emptying my mind of its usual busyness.

Kajedo sees Findhorn as a greenhouse for spirituality and says: "The whole community is like a hothouse where we live in a sheltered and protected environment and grow faster and bigger. A lot of natural processes get intensified here."

Increasingly I hold my thoughts and behaviour up to scrutiny, checking to ensure that I am as kind and loving as I know how to be. This is the Findhorn way.

In the gardens there is a pervasive awareness of the interconnectedness of all life and I share the joy when four swarms of bees unexpectedly arrive and take up residence. Many see it as an answer to their prayers and meditations.

The auspicious happening follows an initiative by 92-year-old Dorothy Maclean, the sole surviving co-founder, who has led weekly meditations dedicated to the well-being of the bees. Around the world, and especially in the northern hemisphere, there has been an alarming dying out of these remarkable creatures which are vital to pollinate much of our food, Albert Einstein predicting that if they were to go, we humans would follow within four years.

I chat to Rona Ribeiro who's very excited by the new arrivals: "These little creatures have a special magic and its fascinating that one bee in its lifetime produces one teaspoon of honey, which is all the human body can digest at one time. Honey shouldn't be seen simply as a sweetener, but rather a life-sustaining medicine.

"Our vision for the garden is to create a sanctuary for the bees where we can offer them acknowledgement, appreciation, nourishment and love. We'd like to establish hives, including one in the original garden, which is an offering strictly for them and not to be harvested for a number of years. And then it would be a case of taking only a fraction of the honey for medicinal purposes."

Her dream is not only to explore what needs to be done to increase and maintain a healthy bee population; but to expand the edible landscape with a thriving fruit tree nursery and to lay the foundations for a 'Spirit in Nature' educational programme focusing on permaculture, forest gardens and medicinal plants. It will include visitors' tours of gardens that are beautiful, edible and medicinal.

"We would love Park Garden to become more of a resource for education not only for our own guests and community, but also for local groups."

Many months earlier I find a beautiful angel figurine in the undergrowth while clearing the site for MoonTree, a purpose-built wooden Eco building fashioned from local and recycled materials that is to be a welcoming space for the gardeners and guests, especially during the cold winter months.

I photograph Rona with the angel for our internal magazine and the picture is spotted by an Italian Experience Week participant who decides her friend and associate Julia Butterfly Hill should become involved in fund raising for MoonTree. Wow, what synchronicity!

Julia is the renowned American environmental activist, writer and poet who stopped loggers in their tracks when she climbed an ancient redwood tree and refused to budge for 738 days.

With Maren and Nathalie and the ornamental pond created in the Original Garden

She agrees to visit Findhorn to share her inspiring message and donates the proceeds of her talk to MoonTree.

Julia is another of the many inspiring people I've met here, making my Findhorn stay so rich. "What do we want our legacy to be," she asks? Her challenge to us all is to turn inspiration into action and uncover the ways in which we can unlock our gifts and transform blocks and challenges into our greatest contributions.

"Each of us is more powerful than we could ever imagine. We are so often just a thought away from having a magical life beyond belief. We are each ancestors of the future, contributing to the vitality and well-being of all those with whom we share this beautiful, sacred life."

Julia, who is the author of the best-selling book *The Legacy of Luna*, says: "I am very grateful that Findhorn is a place for people from all over the world to come, learn, share, and practice living in harmony with the Earth, with each other, and with all life."

A couple of days later another plan comes together when my animal whisperer friend Anna Breytenbach addresses the community and hosts a hugely successful workshop, adding her special gifts to the mix.

Findhorn is a magnet for interesting and unusual people, be they spiritual teachers, artists, musicians or simply seekers of another way of living and being.

CHAPTER TWENTY SEVEN

ANTARCTICA

If Antarctica were music it would be Mozart.
Art, and it would be Michelangelo.
Literature, and it would be Shakespeare.
And yet it is something even greater: the only place on Earth
that is still as it should be. May we never tame it. "

— ***ANDREW DENTON,*** ENTERTAINER AND WRITER

Like many a great gift in my life, it came out of the blue, this time with a tele-phone call from my friend Ferdi de Vos at Toyota South Africa. "Would you like to go to Antarctica?" he asked, knowing my response.

I'd be away for five weeks spanning Christmas and New Year of 2011, finally getting to know that white smudge on the bottom of the world map.

The idea was that I'd journey south from Cape Town aboard the SA Agulhas, South Africa's polar supply and exploration vessel, and write about my experiences. "Oh, and while you are there we'd like you to be a custodian for a Toyota Hilux we are donating to the South African National Antarctica Programme (SANAP). And if you could show the guys how to drive it."

Ferdi made it sound simple, but I was too elated to question the detail. I knew I absolutely had to go, even though I'd taken the seemingly contrary decision to become a pilgrim, walking with a message about treading lightly upon the Earth.

Was I a fraud, I agonized? What would be the implications for my carbon foot-print of a 4,200 km sea voyage, followed by 300 km drive to the SANAE IV base deep within Antarctica, some exploration and training, and then an expensive re-turn flight to Cape Town aboard a Russian cargo aircraft?

Whatever the inconsistencies I knew I had to grab the once-in-a-lifetime chance. Antarctica was the only continent I had not adventured on; it was an opportunity to experience the most pristine part of the planet where the human footprint is lightest; and I'd get paid at a time when my finances were becoming desperate.

What life lessons would I be gifted with? The mission played to my ego-driven quest to always be first among my peers and to maintain a high public profile, but I argued with myself that this was a Godsend, providing a platform for my message as a spiritual and environmental activist.

The breathtaking beauty of the Southern Ocean in mid-summer near the Ice Shelf

Antarctica is the loneliest, coldest, windiest, driest and highest of our seven continents – and arguably the most beautiful, having felt the impact of humans the least.

It is a vast, wild, white wilderness that doesn't belong to any country and has no permanent residents, being home to remarkable creatures like the emperor penguin, leopard seal, snow petrel and wandering albatross that ceaselessly rides the air currents above the neighbouring Southern Ocean.

Antarctica is a giant freezer that is regarded as the thermometer of the planet and a huge laboratory that is unlocking secrets of our past, providing clues to climate change and even glimpses of how conditions might be on a planet like Mars.

Not surprisingly it evokes emotions ranging from abhorrence to rapturous applause, although Norwegian Roald Amundsen, the first man to the South Pole who survived by eating his sledge dogs, declared cynically: "Adventure is just bad planning."

Ironically his rival Robert Falcon Scott found wider fame in the English-speaking world by dying heroically. "Had we lived, I should have had a tale to tell of the hardihood, endurance and courage of my companions which would have stirred the heart of every Englishman," he wrote. "These rough notes and our dead bodies must tell the tale…"

A century later Antarctica continues to inspire, and I was to discover it has a way of getting into your head and your heart and it just won't let go.

The voyage south was a 14-day journey of discovery as I interacted with South Africans of all colours and social stations, sharing a cabin with three tough drivers on loan from the national defence force. They'd been trained to kill and to survive under extreme conditions, but it was their innate kindness, compassion, humour and sense of adventure that I remember most fondly.

Each day brought fresh natural wonders, but perhaps none more spectacular than the colossal blue icebergs that seemed to glow with an inner light; or the lone wandering albatross with its massive wingspan and ability to soar and glide without effort. How does a creature like this survive for months on the wing?

Once, while pondering life from my lofty vantage point in the Monkey Island, I was suddenly filled with a great sense of fear and foreboding, suddenly feeling totally vulnerable and insignificant. If something went wrong, help would be days away, if it came at all. Was I going to die in this inhospitable icescape that is the breeding ground for the worst weather on the planet? My gut churned with fear.

Many of those absurd middle-of-the-night fears surfaced. Conquering them would be part of my journey, I realized, while recognising that this white wilderness brings out the best in people, attracting adventurous souls who are ready to explore the outer limits of their courage. Would I be worthy?

Standing in the bow and watching the reinforced hull crunching and munching its way through the ice I imagined how it must have been when the original supercontinent of Gondwana broke up and formed the world and land masses we know today.

Around 200 million years ago Antarctica was joined with Africa, South America, India, Australia and New Zealand and fossil evidence includes a deciduous conifer, a fern and a terrestrial reptile. Imagine that!

Finally, with a bump, we are up against the Ice Shelf and can begin the dangerous task of unloading heavy equipment, knowing that huge chunks of ice, sometimes kilometres long, can break away at any moment.

Some scientists and researchers remain aboard the ship with the crew, although many will eventually be transported by helicopter to the inland base. As a driver, I find myself clinging precariously on rope netting as I am swung over a menacingly dark, icy sea by a crane mounted on the deck. I'm aware that one tiny slip could be terminal, adding another name to the list of fatalities linked to exploration of our wildest and most inhospitable continent. But somehow the nearness of possible death sharpens our focus and makes life all the more delicious.

Then, with a thud I'm down, gratefully feeling ice and snow beneath huge yel-

**The Ice Truckers with Geoff (on right) at the start of the pioneering drive
to the South African base**

low boots irreverently nicknamed *pumpkin shoes*. Yee-haaaaa! I feel like whooping with joy.

Soon it is the turn of the muscular, high-riding Toyota to be lowered onto the shelf and the fun begins, although my first few moments behind the wheel are hardly auspicious.

Watched and cheered by many aboard the ship, my Antarctic driving debut proves too public for my liking. I realize I still have a huge investment in ego and dread making a fool of myself in such unfamiliar terrain.

I struggle to insert impossibly huge, clunky boots into the driver's foot-well. Luckily it is a two-pedal automatic but my right foot feels numb inside its giant boot and entirely disconnected from the accelerator. I try to prod gently but the revs soar. Finally I'm moving… slowly gathering momentum despite wheelspin on the impossibly slippery surface. Yay! The Toyota edges away from the ice shelf only to sink up to the differentials in very deep snow. I'm stuck with all eyes on me, knowing that I am on trial. My ego doesn't like this one bit and that's of course the first important lesson of the day. Deal with it!

I've never driven under snow conditions this extreme and no conventional 4x4 vehicle has ever ventured to the South African base, the challenging 300 km ice and snow route being the domain of monster vehicles that weigh more than 20 tons and ride on tank-style tracks, rather than tyres.

"We call it slush-puppy snow. It's the worst kind to drive," I'm informed. "You are going to have your work cut out for you." Too true! I get stuck four or five times in the first kilometre, and need a tow from one of the giant Challenger vehicles to get moving again. Embarrassing!

<hr />

A pessimist would have described Day One as a disaster and the head of operations, Shiraan Watson, asks: "Do you think we should load it back on the ship?"

One of his senior colleagues is probably gleeful, having warned me: "I want to see this project fail."

Why, I demand, arguing that similar Toyotas with appropriate modifications have already acquitted themselves as the first and only conventional vehicles to reach both magnetic poles. "Because I wasn't consulted," he admits. Ugh, that male ego again.

He had also been tasked with providing a GPS and an aerial for the vehicle's radio, the GPS proving problematic while there was no sign of the necessary antenna. Without these I could be signing my death warrant if I attempted to drive to the base and the weather turned nasty, the worst case scenario involving whiteout conditions with zero visibility.

I'd also be unable to report my plight or appeal for help without the vital radio antenna. To make matters worse the Toyota is not equipped with any survival gear and normal 4x4 procedure in extreme conditions is always to travel in convoy with at least one other vehicle.

In the end I'm persuaded by the Challenger drivers to delay my attempt for a fortnight and their concerns prove entirely valid. Leaving the Toyota parked; I join the convoy of monster Challengers and share the driving to the SANAE IV base.

Warnings about what could happen are prophetic. We experience several hours in dangerous whiteout conditions where we rely exclusively on GPS technology to keep us from plunging into known crevasses. It scares me silly and I'm all too aware of my sweaty palms on the controls, wiping them often.

But my tutor, Gary Harper, a veteran ice trucker, is calm and reassuring, eventually stretching out on the cramped bunk alongside me and instantly going to sleep. We crawl blindly through the world's deadliest landscape, communicating via vehicle-to-vehicle radios while maintaining identical speeds to avoid collisions within the convoy.

My eyes are riveted on the GPS, rather than the windscreen, as I keep making tiny steering connections to keep the vehicle on course. Sometimes it slides, at other times it lurches wildly over unseen sastrugi to the accompaniment of loud crashing sounds.

I'm unbelievably tense when I hear that small still voice within telling me this is a lesson in faith. I think of the example of the Findhorn community founders and realise this is a perfect test: a chance to live in complete faith. A soothing calm comes over me and I start enjoying the driving.

When a retaining pin on one of the trailers breaks, I'm relaxed. We stop to effect repairs. A vehicle won't restart and there's more tinkering with spanners in an icy blizzard. Twice we refuel in the driving wind and snow.

Eventually, after several hours, we begin to see more than the end of the vehicle's orange bonnet, the base on Versleskarvet (Little Barren Mountain) finally looming into view. It is still more than three hours away as we crawl ant-like across this vast and desolate land. Everything that isn't white seems much closer than it really is and the clarity enables you to see forever!

A direction sign with distances to the North and South Poles, Cape Town and leading Antarctic bases has been partly submerged by recent heavy snowfalls and is the first sign of human habitation in ages.

We've been on the road for 28 nail-biting hours and finally pull up outside the base a little before midnight. It is Christmas Day (the whitest I've ever known) and I've learned a valuable lesson in faith and finesse. Now I can relax and celebrate in the company of heroes.

Two amazing weeks pass before another GPS is located, an antenna installed and it is time to put the Toyota to the test on the 300 km inland route to the base. Conditions are perfect and Mother Nature co-operates with a glorious summer day and mild temperatures between minus 5 and minus 10 degrees Celsius. Positively sublime!

I'm again in the company of the giant Challengers and I run ahead, waiting at pre-arranged waypoints for the convoy to catch up. The Hilux is in its element, proving effortlessly quiet and comfy on its big, soft tyres. Grip is impressive.

Sometimes we negotiate waves of ice sculpted by the wind where the Hilux scatters showers of ice crystals like spume upon the ocean. I feel a sense of oneness with the universe and when I stop and switch off, I can hear my own heartbeat and feel the blood pulsing through my veins.

It is an utterly beautiful white wilderness and the team take extreme measures to minimize their impact on the world's most pristine environment. I'm delighted to learn that all litter is shipped back to South Africa aboard the Agulhas.

Geoff and Shiraan Watson with the Toyota Hilux at the South African base in Antarctica

When we arrive at the lonely caboose that is a halfway emergency shelter and refuelling station, those that need the toilet use a black plastic bag that will find its way home to Cape Town at the end of the summer season. Poo-ing in a bag is a new and uncomfortable experience for me.

The sun is still shining brightly at midnight and we brew coffee with melted snow while my fellow travellers opt for a traditional South African barbecue despite a bitter wind.

At 2am we push on and too soon we're there. At 21 hours it's the fastest-ever traverse by Challenger vehicles and all agree the Toyota could have done it in less than half the time. The Hilux scores again when it takes on 85 litres of polar diesel compared with around 2,000 for the next vehicle.

We've done it. There are handshakes, hugs and high-fives. If the motoring history of Antarctica was a book it would be a slim volume, but the Toyota has written an exciting new chapter. Like Arnold Schwarzenegger in *The Terminator*, I silently vow: "I'll be back."

CHAPTER TWENTY EIGHT

GEOFF-FREE!

Walk gently on Mother Earth. She is the only one we have.
– *ARCHBISHOP EMERITUS DESMOND TUTU*, NOBEL LAUREATE

Everywhere is within walking distance if you have enough time and I've allocated five years, ten years or whatever it takes. I'm 63, superbly healthy and figure I have enough summers left to make a difference.

The idea is simple enough: I'll walk the equivalent of the circumference of the Earth with a message about living simply, sustainably and joyfully without all the stuff we burden ourselves with. Without the car, house, furniture and crammed cupboards that have been part of my life, often possessing me rather than setting me free.

Now, if it doesn't fit in my rucksack, it is of little use. I'm Geoff-free!

And today really is the first day of the rest of my Life. It is July 7, 2011, and a date chosen to honour the memory of Peace Pilgrim, a great source of inspiration who passed on this day 30 years earlier.

Having already met Satish Kumar, editor of *Resurgence* magazine and presenter of BBC's beautiful *Earth Pilgrim* film, reading the story of her life is the clincher. A lightbulb moment! She'd walked for 28 years with a message of peace and touched so many lives.

Besides I figure walking is something almost anybody can do, so with my two feet and my journalistic background I should be able to get a message out to those receptive to different ways of living.

This decision has brought me to the Hebridean Isles of Erraid and Iona to take this giant leap of faith as a wanderer with a purpose.

OK, some friends think I've lost my marbles and who can blame them. Gorgeous blonde TV presenter Melanie Walker, who shared a racecar with me years ago, sends a Facebook message: "You are a loony." I agree. It's funny to witness the transition from petrolhead to pilgrim and from skidmarks to gentle footprints.

Suddenly my life has slowed to walking pace and yet on this day I feel the same nervous fluttering of butterflies in my stomach and heightened sense of awareness I know from motor racing. It reminds me of being strapped into a race or rally car, taking deep slow breaths, the engine revving and eyes and brain anticipating the

Bonnie, Geoff And Tammy at Iona Abbey before the start of the pilgrimage walk

millisecond when the lights turn green or the chequered flag drops, galvanising me into action. Unbelievably exciting and so tense I think I'll implode.

Instead of mashing my right foot down on the accelerator, this time I give my daughters one last hug, take a deep breath and then step forward. The journey of a thousand miles – 25 thousand miles – begins with a single step and mine has just started, unobtrusively observed only by the two people most precious to me.

I'm an apprentice pilgrim with so much to learn and that's fine. I'm up for whatever comes my way. Exhilarated and a little scared, of course.

The worst moment is when the car Bonnie and Tammy are driving disappears from view, following the scenic road from Iona across the Isle of Mull towards mainland Scotland. I have no idea when I'll see them again and that's like being punched in the gut.

In my head I break my journey down into bite-sized chunks so that I'm not overwhelmed by the enormity of the task I've set myself. I don't think about 40,075 km or 25,000 miles. The first leg is from Iona to Findhorn and that's easy for someone who's ticked off Kilimanjaro and Everest Base Camp. Or so I imagine.

It feels so right to be doing what I'm doing, euphoria replacing earlier fears. Maybe this will be less challenging than I imagined. Almost as I think it I feel a hotspot and remove my boot and sock to investigate, the ominous beginnings of a large blister revealing itself. Oh dear, and this is Day One.

**Desmond Tutu provided huge encouragement
with his personal message**

To lift my spirits I think of all my many well-wishers and especially the personal message from Desmond Tutu: "Walk gently on Mother Earth. She is the only one we have. Thank you for reminding us to be reverent and caring for the environment. God go with you." And thank you Father Desmond.

Putting worries about my feet aside, I remember the note Bonnie and Tammy handed me to read later, and feel a lump in my throat. "What you are doing is incredible and fantastic," they assure. "Selfishly we'd like you closer to home and more accessible to us, but we will be wishing you good health, a comfy place to sleep at night, interesting scenery and meetings along the way. What you are doing brings knowledge, love and light to a great cause, the beloved Earth.

"Have fun, be brave and remember that you don't have to suffer, freeze or go hungry to spread your message. Spread your message in true happiness."

The first few days are fun and I delight in spontaneous changes of route and plan. I brave a wet and freezing morning at the lighthouse at Ardnamurchan, the most westerly point in mainland Britain, enjoying perfect weather and panoramic views from the summit of Ben Nevis, the highest point in the land. I marvel at where and how far my feet take me each day.

My concessions to technology – pedometer, smart phone and 10-megapixel pocket camera – capture data and images but tell nothing of the sense of freedom or exhilaration at exploring vast landscapes at a pace our ancestors understood. Or of the wonderful boost I receive with each message of encouragement – I'm not doing this alone.

Nor do the digital readouts reveal anything of the pain, tiredness and occasional longing for the familiar old life and its numbing commitment to speed and comfort. Hey, change is never easy.

On foot we move towards distant horizons in a gentle rhythm that connects instead of severing us from the natural world. I treasure that and realize I now love walking even more than driving, and that was once my passion. There's a sense of the interconnectedness of all life. It is the timeless way of the pilgrim that most people can relate to, even if they choose instead to view their world through windscreens and rear-view mirrors.

"Do you really believe that you can make a difference," I'm asked? Absolutely!

And do I think all this talk of climate change is absolute nonsense? Yes, and the world is flat, although I have great fun debating the point with a tourist in his large luxury motorized camper. We don't agree but get on famously, exchange email addresses and part as pals.

The issues of religion and spirituality are also raised by someone who professes not to believe in God but is clearly in love with life and acknowledges the healing power of nature. Isn't that the same thing? Does it matter what you call divinity?

Walking in nature provides a healing balm although there are difficult moments. Sometimes the pain in my feet and back is excruciating and my body cries out for rest. Once I begin falling asleep while walking in a busy and dangerous single-track road.

On another stretch in the rain I entertain thoughts of what I'd do if a bus came my way. Luckily it is a Sunday and there is no public transport, so I'm not subjected to real temptation.

I laugh often, especially at my predicament when sodden and sore, or attempting to get comfy in the claustrophobia of my waterproof bivvy body-bag that keeps midges out, my sleeping bag dry and me grumpily awake. Only Scotland's notorious blood-guzzling midges threaten a total sense of humour failure.

I think fondly of my friend Inga back home who has taught me to laugh at life. "You were so serious when I first me you," she once admonished.

When I have niggling doubts about my ability to manage a big push on the final day to Findhorn, I silently ask for help. I feel my load lighten and fresh energy course through body, mind and soul. I can hardly feel the weight of my rucksack. Hey, this faith thing really works!

Inga would be delighted to know my last few kilometres to Findhorn are about fun and friendship. Walking between Granton-on-Spey and Forres I see a lone figure striding towards me in the far distance, it eventually morphing into my hiking buddy John Willoner. He's come to greet me a few hours from the end laden with tasty snacks including a fresh fix for this chocoholic.

It's a long day, my trusty pedometer reflecting 10 hours and 36 minutes and 47 km or nearly 30 miles of walking. And the bonus is that I finish on Mandela Day in celebration of the 93rd birthday of the former South African president and world icon. Happy birthday Madiba!

I'm walking again, completing my west-to-east traverse of Scotland when I remember my daughters' entreaty: "Dad, you don't have to suffer…"

The Findhorn-Peterhead leg should be easy but my body is protesting and once, when I hear an anguished whimper, I realized with surprise that it has come from me. Hey, pilgrim, is this the best you can do?

I dream up a *Dark Night of the Soles* headline for my blog and laugh aloud. Yes, I've been taking myself far too seriously, being driven by ego and behaving like a tourist intent on a destination, rather than a pilgrim celebrating each step of the journey. Lighten up, slow down and have fun. And I do.

When a pleasant weariness overtakes me at the end of the day I find an open-fronted World War 2 lookout point on the beach that offers shelter from the rain without obscuring beautiful views over the ocean. I enjoy aloneness without feeling lonely, also trying to imagine what it was like for those young soldiers – now nearly all dead – who manned these coastal defences.

I ponder the futility of war and colossal waste of money and manpower that created mile upon mile of concrete pillboxes and tank traps marching across the coastal landscape.

The next day is rain, rain and more rain and mounting misery as I taunt myself with negative questions. Can I really be the change I wish to see in the world? Is this giant walk just the manifestation of an oversized ego? If I'm treading lightly upon the Earth why do my feet hurt so badly? Then, near the picturesque coastal hamlet of Cullen, my spirits soar again. Former forester Fiona Sutherland, now a healer and mum, comes striding towards me wearing a wide welcoming smile. She and her forester hubby John and young daughters Catriona and Maia have opened their home and hearts to a weary traveller. Just when I need it I'm overwhelmed by the kindness of strangers.

My feet still hurt but I've weathered my Dark Night of the Soul, appreciating that a pilgrim accepts whatever might come and looks for the lesson in every situation, as well as the gift in each person along the way. I in turn hope to be a gift to all I meet.

At the Rattray Head lighthouse and nearby eco hostel I celebrate traversing my first country in the spirit of the ancestors and have fun watching *Forest Gump* for the first time in many years. I chuckle at the scene where he is running coast-to-coast across the US and suddenly decides to quit, throwing an army of self-appointed disciples into confusion.

I'm raring to go again and after catching up with my work at Findhorn I'm off, this time heading southwards from John o' Groats and Dunnet Point, the most northerly bit of Britain.

Dunnet Head is a place of spectacular cliffs, soaring seabirds and wild seas, and it is here that I photograph charismatic young Russian Natasha Krasnikova, without knowing her story. A few hours later we meet by chance in a hostel and she invites me to share her celebratory cheese and wine feast, having hitch-hiked the length of Britain on the greatest adventure of her young life.

I also meet Londoner Anna Hughes who works with a movement which promotes walking and cycling as a way of getting to know your local area.

She's pedalling the entire coastline of Britain. "I love cycling and wanted to see the coast," she explains. You go Girl!

Both Anna and Natasha speak glowingly of a young artist called Frank who's sketched and painted his way across the country. Why didn't he cycle instead of walking, Anna demanded? "Because I don't know how to ride a bike," he admitted honestly. Bravo to so many brave souls.

When I reach the historic Grey Cairns of Camster on a cold, blustery evening, I know I've found a perfect home for the night. This has been a sacred site for 5,000 years, the ancestors creating giant cairns of rocks which housed chambers big enough to accommodate a number of people. Today these rank among the best-preserved cairns of their kind in the British Isles.

I shelter from the wind alongside the biggest one and sleep peacefully, setting off cheerfully at dawn, despite a bitter wind. My gloved hands are so cold they hurt and I remind myself this is technically still summer in Scotland. (Note to self: find better gloves before winter!)

At the hamlet of Berriedale I'm drawn to the peace of the cemetery and adjoining church, enjoying a leisurely snack of fruit and nuts while resting my feet. Hey, I like this place, I think, and wonder if the kindly reverend suspects my intentions when he asks me to close the gate when I leave.

I say a prayer for those still mourning the passing of loved ones and find a quiet, windless corner that traps the last rays of the setting sun. What follows is the comfiest night of camping yet and I'm touched by the sentiment on a nearby gravestone: 'Our loved ones are never more than a thought away.' I think fondly of mine.

The next day I alternate between walking the railway tracks and barefooting it down the beach; taking a dip in a clear stream and lying in the sun to dry in a remote and secluded little bay. I fall asleep and hope the spectacle of a naked wrinklie sunning himself isn't too much for the passengers on a train that suddenly clickety-clacks onto the scene.

It is early days and I'm still taking wobbly, baby steps as an apprentice pilgrim, but this walking thing is addictive.

CHAPTER TWENTY NINE

CAMINO DE SANTIAGO

One's destination is never a place but a new way of seeing things.
—**HENRY MILLER,** WRITER AND ARTIST

The Camino de Santiago first loomed large on my landscape around 1996 when I was handed a book by Brazilian writer Paulo Coelho, eagerly devouring his fantastical word-pictures and later following up with an eccentric pilgrimage account by American screen legend and Oscar winner Shirley MacLaine.

As I recall she spent much of her time in terror of savage dogs, or being pursued by paparazzi, although something resonated within me as from then on it was a question of *when* rather than *if*.

A couple of years later I was sitting in my dressing gown and sipping hot water at a health spa when a vision of vitality and loveliness walked into the room and took my breath away. "I want what you're on. What's your secret?" I asked rather brazenly. I'd never seen anyone looking more radiantly healthy.

"I've just walked the Camino in Spain and only eat raw food," she confided, politely ignoring the fact that I was so openly admiring. Later she admitted that her life in the high-pressure and materialistic fashion world had been in a dangerous downward spiral. She'd lost all sense of perspective and retreated to Spain to slow down and restore her sanity. Now there was no turning back.

I was hooked and increasingly met others who had trod that same medieval trail from France over the Pyrenees and into Spain, traversing the Iberian Peninsula before reaching the cathedral in the city of Santiago de Compostela. In centuries past Santiago rivalled Rome and Jerusalem in importance as a Christian pilgrimage centre, attracting up to half a million people in a Holy Year when the Day of St James – July 25 – fell on a Sunday.

They came on foot from all over Europe, typically wearing a wide-brimmed hat and shoulder cape while carrying a satchel, a walking stick, a gourd filled with water and the scallop shell that is the symbol of St James, one of the apostles of Jesus Christ. One legend is that the original route accessed the lost city of Atlantis while it is widely accepted that pre-Christian travellers forged their way along the same route following the stars and the Milky Way to what was regarded as the end of the world.

By the 1970s the pilgrimage to Santiago was tottering on the brink of extinction; only enjoying a revival quite recently, that peaked in 2010, a Holy Year when 280,000 people obtained a *credencial* identifying them as pilgrims, although many succumbed to the physical and psychological rigours of the walk. A year later 100,000 fewer were anticipated, which suited me fine as I get edgy in crowds. Yes, Santiago was definitely on my 2011 to-do list.

Pilgrims tick their reasons for walking: religious, spiritual, historical or sporting, although it is rarely that simple. Many only fully appreciate the gifts of the Camino much later.

Privately almost everyone volunteers a different explanation, crisis being a catalyst, whether it is the painful disintegration of a relationship, death of a loved one, loss of a job or simply the realisation that there is more to life.

Our modern worlds move at such speed that we could jet to Rome, Jerusalem and Santiago in a day and maybe we all need to slow to the walking pace of our ancestors and reconnect with the natural world around us.

For me the Camino feels like the next logical step on my path as I flex my pilgrim muscles, although there's a delightful interlude first when I cross the skinny bit of England in Cornwall, following St Michael's Way in the company of Adelle, who is tracing her own family roots.

Our footsteps reverberate along ancient cliff paths overlooking golden beaches; explore historic settlements and lead us across farmlands and past standing stones that have been sacred markers for thousands of years. They end at St Michael's Mount, a spectacular granite outcrop rising from the sea that has been home to Benedictine monks for centuries. I'm delighted to discover that it is one of many pilgrim routes that ultimately links to Santiago, the trail even featuring the signature seashell emblem.

Just days later, after a smooth ferry crossing from the south of England to Spain, I'm to realize that pilgrim paths, tracks and roads converge on Santiago from all over Europe with new hostels and facilities springing up each year to accommodate the surge in seekers.

My Camino officially begins before dawn when I set off from the imposing monastery in Roncesvalles; walking alone as I temporarily leave Spain and begin meeting *peregrinos* huffing and puffing their way towards me from France. There is no border or passport check.

Seeing the scallop shell hanging from my rucksack, one exclaims: "You're going the wrong way, Friend. Santiago is the other way." Amusement turns to astonishment when I laugh and explain that I'll re-trace my steps the next day after meeting a friend in St Jean Pied de Port. "Twice across the Pyrenees. Are you mad?"Why not? I love walking and especially in the mountains on a bright, sunny day.

Am I making this double journey out of kindness to a friend with no serious walking experience, I wonder, or driven by the primal mating instinct? We'd met in Findhorn a few weeks earlier and there was a definite attraction, she unexpectedly following me, perhaps remembering the promise of a lingering goodnight kiss.

Albergues or pilgrim hostels can be wonderfully welcoming although rarely conducive to romance, crowding as many single bunk beds as practical into a large room. So the first couple of days are an agony of sexual tension, allowing me time to examine my motives.

Am I falling into a familiar trap? The important thing isn't to pursue this relationship, I decide, even though it has started promisingly enough. I need to focus and consolidate my pilgrim credentials by walking mindfully and continuously. I suspect there'll be important lessons during solo time along with insights from like-minded souls.

The ego part of me wants to tick off another country, Spain being a lot wider than Scotland and auspicious as the only ancient pilgrimage walk with world heritage status. She, meanwhile, is fantasising about a comfy hotel and some rest days.

But I'm into my stride. I was born to walk. We all are. I'm loving the Camino and enjoying an important attitudinal shift. Each step needs to be a prayer and a blessing, honouring the Earth. I feel that deep within and the toughest thing on the first few days is wearing a shirt I've gaudily emblazoned with my website address *www.earthpilgrimafrica.com*

It renders me exposed, conspicuous and self-conscious and fulfils its purpose, attracting questions, curiosity, surprise, sometimes even gratitude. "Thank you for doing this for us."

With each day my urge to crawl into my lady friend's bunk is diminished. What I need is solo time, while her body is crying out for a less punishing routine. The inevitable happens and we part, not knowing if we'll meet again. Or want to.

Other friends take her place alongside me, respectfully honouring my choice to walk in silence for the first hour or two until after sunrise. It is my favourite time when I sense my oneness with creation and marvel at the colours in God's palette. The Camino is already everything I'd dared hope and gets better each day as my body adapts to new rhythms.

The final few days are magical. Not only do I discover some superbly welcoming hostels, but I am again in the company of favourite *peregrinos*. It is part of the normal ebb and flow that even the closest of friends, walking at their own pace, often separate for days and sometimes never connect again.

Deciding on an early start for the final trek to Santiago I step outside to be greeted by an invigorating chill and an inky-black sky sprinkled with bright stars – and there, my familiar friend Jupiter waits to confirm my way West. Magically the rain and clouds of recent days have vanished to make way for a perfect dawn.

With me are two of my most cherished pilgrim pals, petite Susanne, a 32-year-old German neuro-psychologist, and Joni, a tall dramatically handsome 33-year-old Finnish minstrel who sets hearts aflutter, not all of them female. An award-winning chef asks Joni to help him serve guests their dinner, and says proudly to me: "It is like having Brad Pitt in my kitchen."

Susanne, Joni and I walk in companionable silence, some considerable distance apart, each cherishing quiet time with our thoughts. Occasionally I click on my headtorch to look for Camino signs, the familiar seashell emblem having guided us faithfully more than 800 km since starting in France 28 days earlier.

Heading into forest, a carpet of autumn leaves muffles our footsteps and the usual hypnotic clicking of my trekking poles, while tall trees crowd above to block out much of the starlight. Owls hoot mournfully and seem to be asking their own searching questions about the meaning of life. Who? Who?

Gradually the sky is painted in the delicate pastel shades of the dawn, revealing droplets of water gleaming like precious strands of jewels in spider web necklaces.

Pilgrims Joni Paavilainen and Susanne Verbiesen with Geoff on the Camino de Santiago in Spain

It is heart-wrenching in its beauty and still Mother Nature has more; a fine mist rolling in to complete the magic and mystique.

I've already decided to dedicate this momentous day to the Findhorn community in northern Scotland, inwardly honouring the individuals and the collective who have been such a source of inspiration in my searching. Many have become valued friends.

I also run through checklists of people and things I'm grateful for, remembering loved ones, even if I can't physically be with them for birthdays or gatherings.

Days earlier I celebrate the birthday from afar of Inga who has taught me to laugh at myself and at life.

My pal Nigel Everingham, an attorney with a wicked sense of deadpan humour, clocks 60 and with each click of my sticks I say Thank You – the trekking poles are a present from Nigel and his wife Jenny.

I feel warmed by all the love despite that biting cold that is most intense around sunrise and spot a friendly café just when my hands are beginning to lose all feeling. I wrap them around a hot chocolate, my new favourite daytime drink. There is animated chatter and music playing – *I shot the Sheriff* is a song from another world and time!

Santiago gradually looms into view, the skyline a far cry from what greeted fellow pilgrims in the Middle Ages. Then the cathedral would have beckoned from afar whereas today it is partially hidden by modern buildings until you are almost upon it.

Arriving in the Old City I thrill to that familiar sense of religious awe I first felt as a child visiting Gaudi's masterpiece, the Sagrada Familia church in Barcelona. Entering Santiago's famous Prado Obradoiro with its ensemble of historic buildings is a moment to eclipse even that encounter, rivalling my first exploration of the Vatican. I momentarily forget my cynicism about an organisation rooted in power, wealth and dogma that has been responsible for so much bloodshed.

St James was a humble Galilean fisherman but in the telling and retelling of the legend he becomes a terrifying Christian soldier on horseback, slaying the Moors as he helps defend and recapture Spain from the grasp of Muslim invaders.

I'm not too sure about him although the cathedral wins me over. It is magnificent and to make the day complete I meet more friends I'd lost contact with along the way, all of us enjoying the ritual of getting our *credencial* pilgrim passport stamped.

We are congratulated and awarded a Compostela, which apparently assures time off in Purgatory. It feels good receiving the certificate, even though I'll probably discard it later.

I bump into Morgan, a 21-year-old Australian with a zest for life, and we excitedly compare notes. His youthful energy is infectious.

Today I love everybody and my joy is complete when we all gather for an al fresco dinner around the corner from the cathedral, Susanne generously inviting me to share the luxury of her hotel room. I'm touched.

At breakfast in another animated café we are joined by Irish gardener Paul who has impressed with his calm stoicism despite considerable suffering. He is looking lean and assured, where earlier he questioned his ability to continue through the pain.

Many attend the famous Noon mass but my focus is already on Finisterre and the end of the Earth.

Susanne and Paul stroll with me to the outskirts of the Old City until it is time for final embraces. I feel an incredible rush of love, seeing the sacred in all around me. It is a precious moment.

I grab a last glance at the cathedral, wondering about the saint whose mortal remains were reportedly rediscovered in a cave in this region. How they got here from Jerusalem centuries after he was executed remains a mystery. Believe what you like.

I try and imagine what each of my friends has got from the Camino experience. None are staunch Catholics believing their sins will be forgiven and the slate wiped clean, although all are seekers of one sort or another. If nothing else they're fitter and have enjoyed a surprisingly cheap holiday.

How intriguing though that every hamlet along the way boasts an impressive church, although so many are now mostly locked and inaccessible to pilgrims other than during mass or formal services. Instead the innumerable bars, cafes and restaurants lining the Camino routes have become the informal meeting places for *peregrinos*.

Today I leave most of my fellow pilgrims behind as I walk less-travelled paths to Finisterre, following in the footsteps of ancestors who navigated by the stars. I relish a more solitary opportunity to integrate all the insights and lessons of the past month.

Allocating three days to cover around 100 km my big surprise arrives on the second day when I find myself staggering in high winds that threaten to topple me over, while driving rain penetrates everywhere. I'm exhausted and my hands so cold they barely function.

I enter a bar, leaving a wet trail to the counter, and order a hot drink; only to discover my hands are too numb to tear open the sachet of drinking chocolate, spilling much of it. Then I lack the co-ordination to stir the drink and eventually just cup it between my palms, gratefully enjoying the warmth.

Geoff reaches Finistere which was once regarded as the end of the world by early pilgrims

Why not book into the *albergue* next door, the proprietor wisely suggests – and it's the best idea I've heard in ages. I didn't realize there was a hostel nearby and recognize that I'm not my best. I've walked only part of the distance I planned, but appreciate the logic in getting warm and dry. And in allowing an extra day to reach Finisterre!

Others have a similar idea and we build a fire to dry our clothes and then have a marvellous shared meal of vegetable soup, pasta, bread and local wine.

I head out the next morning feeling revitalized, hardly noticing the weight of my pack. Even the familiar pains in my feet are diminished. It's a high point and the best is to come when I reach Finisterre and then eagerly stride to the lighthouse at the tip of a rocky promontory jutting into a wild, windswept Atlantic ocean.

It's the final countdown and I reach a mileage marker that reads 0.00 km. The setting is the most beautiful I've seen in Spain and reminds me of South Africa's celebrated Cape Point, which prompted navigator Sir Francis Drake to enthuse: "The fairest cape we saw in the whole circumference of the Earth".

Ignoring a wind that makes standing at the edge of the cliffs dangerous, I suck in fresh salt sea-air and ponder the lessons of my 34-day, 1,018km odyssey. Whatever the reasons for walking I feel sure the Camino always delivers special gifts.

A fundamental problem of our modern world, I decide, is the disease of disconnection. We've become disconnected from each other, the natural world and the Creator. We're mired in materialism.

One of my most haunting Camino experiences was in the pre-dawn darkness when I heard ethereal music floating towards me from a roadside shrine in a tiny village. It was breathtakingly moving, touching me in the same way Mozart or *Ave Maria* does.

I think many pilgrims expect a profound mystical experience, perhaps seeing a bright beam of light from the heavens as they enter Santiago – and maybe it is like that for some.

A friend comments that his lesson is that everything he needs is offered. He has food, water, shelter, companionship, inspiration and unexpectedly discovers love along the way.

My Camino is confirmation that a simple life can be utterly joyful and inspiring. And it is about the spark of divinity I see in others and the realization that the light in the eyes I'm looking out of - and into - is God's light.

CHAPTER THIRTY

EXPECT A MIRACLE

*Never doubt that a small group of concerned
citizens can change the world. Indeed,
it is the only thing that ever has.*
— *MARGARET MEAD,* ANTHROPOLOGIST

As gale-force winds rage around me and rain and sleet batter the window panes, I can think of no more compelling or inspiring place to see in the New Year of 2012 than the secluded Traigh Bhan retreat centre on the sacred Hebridean Isle of Iona.

It's wild and beautiful outside, the wind whipping up spray from the wave tops, while inside I'm warm and snug in an oasis of tranquillity as I focus on a candle flame and commit to the year ahead.

The world is changing dramatically all around me and I give thanks for that momentum – and thanks also to be an active member of the Findhorn Foundation community as it commemorates and celebrates 50 years as a force for positive change and new ways of living harmoniously and sustainably.

It was on November 17, 1962 that founders Dorothy Maclean and Peter and Eileen Caddy and their three young sons first arrived at The Park in Findhorn with their now-famous caravan in tow, little realising that they were the nucleus of a spiritual community that would become synonymous around the world with transformation and a commitment to awakening the highest in human potential.

A half century later it is a place of inspiration to me and so many others as an ongoing and evolving social experiment and a striving for a higher consciousness. And like Iona it is perceived as a power point upon the Earth and part of a global 'network of light'. Significantly Traigh Bhan, which means 'White Strand' in Gaelic, was bought that same year by Jessica Ferreira and used as a sanctuary from which to radiate love and blessings out into the world.

In 1971, when Jessica was approaching her 80s, she gifted the retreat home to Findhorn newlyweds Katherine and Roger Collis. They felt the gift of the house and sanctuary was for a wider purpose to be made available to the many people who would be called to Iona in the future. They arranged for the deed to be transferred to the Findhorn Trust, ensuring it remains an intimate extension of the community in perpetuity.

Just days earlier I'd met the couple at Findhorn as they prepared to celebrate their 40th wedding anniversary and I marvelled at their generosity and selfless contribution to a community they love and continue to serve, even though they no longer live there.

Call it serendipity or whatever you like, but a last-minute cancellation means I can be on Iona over New Year, quietly taking stock of my life and writing final chapters for this book. It was here in the Sanctuary at Traigh Bhan, with its perfect views across to the neighbouring Isles of Mull and Erraid; that I joined a meditation six months earlier before starting my walking pilgrimage.

So much has happened in the interim, and I suspect the coming year of walking in the US will be as profound.

Sitting in the Sanctuary I listen to the wind and rain while a song written by former Findhorn songbird Elizabeth Rogers plays in my head:

Yes, life begins now, it's time to learn how, to set yourself free
It's yours to create, don't stop there and wait, it's time to dive in
Tomorrow could be too late, don't hesitate, just breathe and begin...

There is no time like now and her song feels like a clarion call to action, somehow also reminding me of the remarkable happenings around the world in recent months as ordinary people reclaim their power, challenging the control of the planet's resources by a wealthy few.

History has shown that what is right will eventually triumph, obvious lessons including the abolition of slavery, growth of the civil rights movement and dismantling of *apartheid*. More recently governments and dictatorships have toppled and we've seen the rise of the Occupy movement, which has as its slogan: "You can't evict an idea whose time has come."

In my own life I've seen the cruel discriminatory ideology of *apartheid* dismantled, joyfully witnessing the world's most famous prisoner walking to freedom.

So I'm optimistic about the future and our next great challenge to reverse the ecocide that threatens the health of land, water, air and all lifeforms through the destruction and loss of ecosystems – all because of greed and a reckless lust for material wealth.

Barrister Polly Higgins has proposed to the United Nations that ecocide be recognized in international law as a threat to peace along with genocide, crimes against humanity, crimes of aggression and war crimes.

**Jonathan Caddy is perpetuating the Findhorn tradition
of living in faith**

In an article in *Resurgence* magazine she argues: "Take away the very world that feeds us and gives us all that we need to live in peace and harmony, and very soon we too will perish. Our right to life is under threat of being extinguished and yet we continue to ignore the signs.

"The very land we call our home is sacred. All too easily it is squandered for the profit of a few at the expense of the wider Earth community."

Thank goodness for visionaries like Polly and thanks also for all those people working individually and collectively for the common good. I find many of them around me at Findhorn where I admire a lack of dogma and a willingness to engage all the issues that confront 21st century soul travellers.

I believe we can also contribute by living as simply and as sustainably as we know how, the community already acknowledged for one of the lowest recorded ecological footprints in the developed world.

Since creating a base at Findhorn my life has certainly changed and my carbon footprint shrunk radically. For the first time since I was a teenager I've managed without owning a car, driving only rarely, although it remains one of my pleasures. If somebody needs a lift to and from Inverness Airport, I'm up for it if they have access to wheels.

It amuses me greatly that in my previous world as a jet-setting motoring journalist I could drive almost any new car I wished and wherever I chose. Now I'm in demand as a volunteer car parking attendant whenever there is a big function in the Universal Hall. Back in South Africa car guards are mostly impoverished black refugees who can't find other employment.

And instead of being insulated in a metal, glass and plastic motorised cocoon, I walk or cycle almost everywhere, delighting in the fact that my feet take me so far, so efficiently. It is a gift to live in a fit and healthy body.

As a volunteer I've enjoyed contributing in two departments – Communications and Park Garden – alternating between serving as a journalist and a gardener. The latter has really connected me with the Earth and the cycles of the seasons, my focaliser Rona Ribeiro understanding the healing benefits of being close to the soil. "Come and be in the garden whenever you need its nurturing," she urges.

Most of my meals are taken in the company of friends in the Community Centre and all are vegetarian with much of the produce grown organically in neighbouring gardens lovingly tended by community members and visitors alike. It's so exciting to eat healthy food that was harvested only hours earlier.

On Christmas Day I'm mildly uncomfortable to see that turkey is an option, although I resolve to make no judgements. A month later haggis is served during an annual celebration of the life of Scots poet Robert Burns, but for the other 363 days of the year the menu is strictly vegetarian.

Moral issues aside, I believe that if we wish to tread more lightly, one of the best things we can do is eradicate or reduce our meat consumption and especially our intake of beef. I guess most of us know that.

Findhorn feels like a healthy place to be physically, psychologically and spiritually. It sits on a narrow peninsula and now that military operations at neighbouring RAF Kinloss have been drastically scaled down it is more peaceful. I am enjoying the blessings of abundant fresh water, clean fresh air from the adjoining North Sea and Moray Firth, a sustainable supply of wood for heating, low population numbers and so many people who are such good company.

Of the original founders, 92-year-old Dorothy Maclean is the sole survivor, and it is a privilege to enjoy her wisdom and friendship. She's getting forgetful about what happened this morning or yesterday, although she has astonishing clarity and vision about the things that matter.

I love Dorothy to bits and am aware she's the same age my mother would be, if she were still around. When my daughters Bonnie and Tammy come to visit, she happily joins the welcoming barbecue for them and is up for many social events, inspiring us with her humour and determination. Using two sticks and resting frequently, she walks every day come wind, rain, sleet or snow. "I'm a Canadian, I love the snow," she explains.

When she publishes her latest book *Memoirs of an Ordinary Mystic* I'm honoured to photograph her for the cover, capturing a moment when she appears youthful and mischievous.

The only other person around who was also there in 1962 is Jonathan Caddy, son of the famous founders, who was born in the original caravan before the move to Findhorn.

Quiet and unassuming, he is a schoolteacher who impresses hugely with his energy, commitment and determination, his guided community walks in the Scottish hills being the stuff of legends. On one Sunday we unexpectedly walk for 12 hours, staggering in exhausted at around midnight. Jonathan is entirely unrepentant, believing it important to push boundaries.

Findhorn 'babes' Gabrielle, Biz and Catriona are the new generation

I love his spirit of adventure and together we've pored over maps, excitedly discussing hikes while Jonathan has been a great source of encouragement with my walking pilgrimage. "I'm with you each step of the way," he once assured, admitting that soon he'd love to undertake a mammoth walking adventure of his own.

His great challenge recently has been to help manifest the dream of Duneland, a low-impact community housing development in the dunes at the end of the Runway that serves as the community's main street. He sees it manifesting as a contemporary example of the power of faith that has underpinned the community for so long.

"Talking about faith is easy to do," he says, "but the Duneland project has yet again required everyone involved to actually put this vital quality into practice. For me this has brought a far deeper respect for the endeavours of my parents and the early pioneers of this community. It is a community that continues to demonstrate a simple and practical way of living and has created a modern transformative myth that has great power and relevance in this materialistic and unstable world that we live in."

Owning a home at Duneland or anywhere else within the community is out of my financial reach, my dwindling Rands earned in South Africa not stretching to a sought-after Findhorn address. But I have faith that my needs will always be met.

All the major buildings have appeared as a lesson in the power of faith, the founders following inner guidance to create pivotal structures like the Sanctuary, Community Centre and Universal Hall, despite the fact that initially they had neither the money nor the numbers to justify the investments in time, talent and resources.

Imagine creating a kitchen and community centre for 200 people when there were only a handful of you, and yet that is exactly what happened when Eileen's guidance said that was what was needed.

"There was no money but we went ahead anyway and the people came," he recalls.

Aerial photographs from the 1970s show a bleak and barren dunescape whereas the latest images feature forest and lush gardens dotted with attractive energy-efficient eco homes, replacing the cramped old caravans that were bitterly cold and expensive to heat.

Jonathan delights in Findhorn as a place of transformation, pointing to the ever-evolving outer landscape and the far-reaching changes that individuals experience during their stay, be it a week or a lifetime.

Conversation with early residents provides an amazing glimpse into a pioneering community that consisted of a number of middle-aged and rather stiff-upper-lip Britons in tweed jackets and conservative dresses who warmly welcomed young arrivals, even if they were long-haired hippies of the love and peace revolution of the 1960s. As long as you were willing to work you had a role.

"It was extraordinary how a group of young hippies in their early 20s were meeting a group of people our parents' age without a hint of separation or alienation," says Angus Marland, who looks back on a 40-year-association after first settling in Findhorn in 1972 as a 22-year-old wood carver and spiritual seeker.

"The place is just as exciting and full of potential now as it was then. What is manifesting now is as important as it was in the late 1960s and early 1970s.

"I came for a weekend visit that turned into a decade."

Many, like Alan Watson Featherstone, go about their business quietly but are examples to us all.

Alan is a diminutive figure with a giant dream to help reverse the catastrophic global trend towards deforestation. With just one percent of Scotland's Caledonian Forest surviving, his long-term goal encompasses an expansive 250-year vision for the return of wild forest to a target area of 600 square miles.

And that healing restoration will be accompanied by a reintroduction of mammal species that flourished when much of the Highlands were densely forested – long before the landscape was transformed into what has been described as a 'wet desert'.

He says the restoration will provide for extensive tracts of majestic Scots pine interspersed with birch, rowan, juniper and aspen trees, recreating a natural environment where beaver, wild boar, lynx and wolf might roam again.

While it has taken many centuries to reduce parts of the Scottish Highlands to their present barren and impoverished condition, elsewhere on the planet – and especially in the life-sustaining tropical rainforests – the accelerated degradation and species loss has happened in our lifetimes and mostly during the past three decades.

If Alan's dream seems audacious, consider that it is already being translated into breathtaking reality and as I write this plans are being finalized for the planting of the millionth seedling by Trees for Life, the award-winning Scottish charity of which he is the founder and executive director.

"Our vision is to restore a wild forest, which is there for its own sake, as a home for wildlife and to fulfil the ecological functions necessary for the wellbeing of the land itself.

"We are not aiming to regenerate a forest which will be utilised sustainably as an extractive resource for people, although we recognise the need for this," he says. "We endorse the efforts of other organisations in seeking to establish a new ecologically sustainable system of forestry, but we strongly believe that this utilitarian approach must be complemented by the restoration of large areas of wild forest."

Are his goals realistic? "I'm an optimist," he insists. "I wouldn't be at Findhorn if I wasn't. My deep-rooted sense of personal optimism for the future stems largely from my personal experience of having access to an unlimited source of inner power – the passion for what I really care about and believe in.

"I've found that I, like any individual, have the power to effect meaningful change in the world. By giving voice to the deepest feelings of my heart and finding ways to express those through practical and positive action, I've discovered previously unknown skills and abilities within myself, and that I can make a difference far beyond my immediate surroundings."

My closest friends at Findhorn are schoolteacher John Willoner and his partner Sylvia Black, who've embraced me with warmth and kindness.

John is probably the most modest and generous person I know, although there is a steely determination there too. He's my hiking buddy and I'm in awe of the fact that he has stood on the summit of all 283 Munros, the highest peaks in Britain, revisiting some many times.

Like so many others since, John was inexplicably drawn to Findhorn, first visiting after receiving a postcard sent by a friend that featured the Findhorn Bay Caravan Park and a cryptic message on the back: "I think you'll find it interesting here."

"I saw a rubbish dump and lots of dilapidated caravans and was looking for site number 27 which was out of sight from the rest, in a hollow. Eventually I found a friend who I'd been at university with and he was with an older person called Peter Caddy who I was introduced to. They were smashing rocks to create a base for a bungalow that was due a couple of months later at Easter. I was given a sledgehammer and joined in."

John only stayed a couple of hours that time but was given some copies of Eileen Caddy's guidance that he found inspiring, and returned often for longer periods until he quit his teaching job down south. That winter of 1967 there were just seven of them but by the end of 1974 the numbers had swelled to between 250 and 300 people.

What was the attraction? "I really enjoyed the company of the three founders – there was some sort of magnetism that's difficult to pinpoint. I enjoyed being in this place that was gradually growing up around the first caravan and had no wish to be anywhere else.

"Peter taught, not in a lecturing way, but while digging alongside him there were pearls of wisdom," John recalls.

Often John can be found practising random acts of kindness, most recently creating a series of seats around The Park so that Dorothy can rest easily during her daily walks, as she tires more quickly these days.

I feel so much richer for knowing people like John, Dorothy, Jonathan and so many others in this open-hearted community. Findhorn has been likened to a beacon of light in a troubled world and for me the greatest gift is the love that shines so brightly and the ongoing demonstration of the power of faith and manifestation. When you join Experience Week, a card in the information folder invites you to "Expect a Miracle."

CHAPTER THIRTY ONE

LOST AND FOUND

Life is what happens while you are busy making other plans.
— *JOHN LENNON,* MUSICIAN

My idea to walk in California is somehow symbolic of my life's larger journey. As crazy as it might seem I decide to start from Los Angeles, the epicentre of money, materialism and car-culture and stride northwards into the welcoming embrace of nature with my message about treading lightly and more lovingly upon the Earth.

It is also a journey through time from my car-worshipping days as a young student hanging out in Hollywood to the places of peace and natural beauty that stir my soul these days, and is representative of my transformation from petrolhead (or motorhead as the Americans would prefer) to pilgrim.

Having accepted Gandhi's challenge to 'be the change you wish to see in the world' I figure that this could also be my ultimate test as I confront motorway madness and a society worshipping at the altar of materialism. Bigger is better, it seems, and I'm surrounded by obesity, whether it be bellies hanging over waistbelts or cars, pickup trucks and motor homes so gargantuan they look like caricatures of themselves.

I start striding, knowing that each step will deepen my inner journey and bring me closer to my eventual geographic goals of some of the most imposing trees on Earth. California is home to redwoods that are the tallest trees on the planet, sequoias that are the largest by volume, and bristlecone pines that are the oldest living things to be found anywhere.

If my shoes hold out, and my 90-day visa is enough, I'll hopefully also visit the legendary High Sierras and Death Valley, the hottest place this side of Hell!

Happily I've never doubted my need for radical change and never for a nanosecond thought of going back to that old life, or else the psychological torture of those first few days might have forced me to quit walking and head instead for the bus stop.

I need to experience and understand this madness though, subjecting myself to a battering by the passage of speeding vehicles, their drivers invariably staring fixedly ahead without expression. Have aliens turned these Earthlings into zom-

Communing with California's ancient Bristlecone Pines that are the oldest trees on Earth

bies devoid of thought and reasoning? Have I wandered onto the set of a Spielberg movie?

Buddha could apparently meditate in a crowded marketplace but I wonder how he'd shut out the mania of the LA freeway system. I can't, reeling with mental and physical exhaustion.

In the first fortnight of walking north I never once receive a wave or smile, or even any meaningful eye contact. Are they afraid that what I have might be contagious? Or perhaps if they look deep into the soul of another being they might become involved; maybe even care for the plight of another.

Finally leaving Highway 101 and joining the more relaxed and scenic Highway 1 is a breath of fresh air, literally and figuratively. I can feel my heartbeat again and hear myself think, which a long walk allows plenty of time for.

Friends and family have said prayers for me and before setting off from LA I visit the Wayfarers Chapel at Palos Verdes that set the scene for this adventure, filling me with joy and expectation. It is the most inspiring modern church I've been in and is made almost entirely of glass, serving as a memorial to Emanuel

Swedenborg, an 18th century mystic and theologian who celebrated the interconnectedness of all life and respected differences and other religious traditions.

Designed by Lloyd Wright, son of renowned American architectural pioneer Frank Lloyd Wright, it is inspired by the majesty of the redwood trees in northern California and those trees that surround the chapel, dominating and creating a sense of the wonder and immensity of the universe.

The entreaty to visitors is: "Pause for a moment, Wayfarer, on life's journey. Let the beauty of holiness restore your soul. May the harmony of sky and water, leaf and rock, nourish the creation and growth of your inner being as you fare through this life and on into the life beyond."

The first Californian night in my sleeping bag is wondrous beneath a canopy of stars and a magnificent full moon, although the rumble of nearby traffic intrudes and competes with the roar of jets overhead on a busy flight path to LAX Airport. I'm also cold, uncomfy and sleep eludes me. Hey, but who's complaining? A pilgrim accepts whatever is.

The further my feet take me from the city, the better it gets, especially alongside the ocean where navigation is simple: keep the sea on the left and one foot in front of the other.

Often I'm moving by 5.30am and one sublimely calm morning the early golden light illuminates dolphins patrolling the shoreline, their sleek aerodynamic bodies gleaming like priceless jewels.

It had to happen though and eventually I'm caught in a Catch 22 situation of being a pedestrian in a car-based society. Highway becomes freeway and warning signs steer me off the main thoroughfare. The only way north is to a naval base where I'm again blocked by officialdom. "You have to have a car around here," the guard explains, stating the obvious.

Joe, a gentle navy man, offers me a lift in his pickup truck and tells me he'll soon be 38 and able to retire after 20 years in uniform, heading back East. "It is too fast-paced and unfriendly here," he laments. "My Dad's also retiring and I'm looking forward to being home, in forests and working with wood. It's very meditative, sort of like walking," he says, thoughtfully eyeing my trekking poles.

He drops me away from the freeway and turns out to be but the first of many kindly souls I'm to meet on a journey I could never have anticipated.

In the space of days my pilgrimage takes me from Tinsel Town and mainstream America to an often-shadowy world of heartache, broken dreams and disillusionment.

Unexpectedly and without conscious choice I cross some unseen divide and find myself among homeless people who've lost all faith in the Great American Dream.

I realize with mild amusement that despite my clean short hair and freshly shaved cheeks, carrying a heavy backpack can brand me not as a hiker, but a homeless person to some.

"We're not homeless; just residentially challenged," a newfound friend quips. Most of his peers are driven by economic circumstance, a handful by choice.

Brett is at the extreme end of this shabby, informal community. He's dirty, disheveled, sun-damaged and missing most of his teeth, but offers to share his meagre food supply and makes me a gift of a tide table that includes the cycles of the moon. It's invaluable.

He recognizes a novice to living on the fringe of society, explaining where I can camp for free and how I should avoid trouble with the authorities and any campers who are drinking heavily. "Rummage in the garbage for a couple of those large black plastic bags," he suggests. "They'll keep you warm and dry."

I feel like a fraud for not admitting that I have an expensive waterproof bivvy bag to keep me and my sleeping bag dry. Sure, I've given up most of my worldly possessions and yet I have so much compared to him, including the lifeline of a credit card.

The irony also isn't lost on me that I'm walking with a message about treading lightly upon our beautiful Earth while Brett and others are doing exactly that, consciously or otherwise. Their ecological footprints leave barely a trace in the dust.

For days I've trudged past beachfront mansions that are monuments to conspicuous consumption, each wearing a prominent warning sign: *No Trespassing – violators will be prosecuted*. How revealing about the disconnection between us. And how interesting that there are more unoccupied holiday homes than homeless people here!

I camp a couple of cold nights with two homeless Army veterans who invite me to share their campfire. Bob is a 64-year-old Vietnam vet with serious leg injuries who looks a little past his sell-by date, his diet a cocktail of painkillers, cigarettes and booze. His friend David is a 53-year-old cancer survivor with a wonderfully probing mind and a love of the outdoors. We get on immediately.

When I talk to Bob about his health, he declares: "When the Good Lord comes to fetch me, I'll be ready. And smoking is the least of my problems!" He needs major heart surgery but seems in no hurry to bare his chest to the medical profession. I'd be scared too.

David admits that he sometimes feels isolated and recognises that this is probably a legacy of his Dad's suicide. "Our church-going neighbours prevented their children from playing with me, fearing that the apple would fall too close to the tree.

"We have a church on every corner but we're pretty Godless," he says.

He's anything but and inspires me with his penetrating insights. He sees trees and especially the lofty redwoods as an antenna between heaven and earth, insisting that in the outdoors he feels the interconnectedness of all things.

David lives on a modest disability pension and says he doesn't miss his ex-wives, house, van, car and motorcycle.

Staring into the campfire, he recalls with sadness: "I've slept by rivers, streams and creeks and they're all polluted. You can't drink the water. We've ruined everything."

But he finds solace and delight in the unexplained mysteries of life and the unseen realms, recognizing that there is a guiding intelligence behind everything. When I bid him goodbye I feel a real sense of loss and he thanks me profusely for giving him some ideas he'll research at a public library. Have homeless people become my community?

In the beautiful city of Santa Barbara that I last visited years ago at the wheel of a powerful sports car while a media guest of General Motors, I ask directions of a lady in an electric wheelchair. She has lost the use of one side of her body and explains: "People wave at me but I just have to smile back as I need my one good hand to drive this thing."

She takes me on a wonderful tour of the downtown area where she has lived all her life and escorts me to the library where I catch up on my emails and the wonders of Google Earth.

I meet more delightful people in the nearby town of Ojai that has been a mecca for spirituality for much of the past century and is seen by many as a cradle for a new human consciousness.

It is here that spiritual luminaries like J Krishnamurti discovered a landscape and an unmistakable energy where people could stop their day-to-day busyness and go into retreat, emerging refreshed with an ability to see life anew.

Krishnamurti welcomed visitors from around the world who were drawn by his penetrating inquiries into the fundamental questions of life, among them writer and satirist Aldous Huxley, screen legend Greta Garbo, Theosophist and women's rights activist Annie Besant, comic actor Charlie Chaplin, quantum physicist David Bohm, novelist D H Lawrence and The Beatles.

Recognising a stranger, people stop and ask if I need any help, one gorgeous young blonde mother proffering her mobile phone, in case I need to make a call. Ojai is evidence that smaller and slower is often friendlier and that some places are imbued with a special energy.

I feel it again when I enter the town of Cambria and joy bubbles up within me. How interesting that, just days earlier, I'd slipped into a dark place when I was completely weary with the lemming-like migration of speeding motorists.

A pilgrim's job is to rouse people from apathy and make them think, but how do you do that when they're seemingly oblivious to your existence?

I'd found myself gloomily judging America as the most wasteful, resource-hungry and regulated society I'd encountered, deciding its citizens had forfeited their freedoms to the giant corporations that control their destiny.

I pondered the message 'In God we Trust' that is enshrined in the constitution and memorialized on dollar bills, when most put their faith in the quest for ever more, the bigger the better. Hey smile Pilgrim and don't go down that negative road.

But something wonderful was now happening. The fact that like energy attracts like energy was playing out before my eyes as I suddenly found myself among so many rejoicing in nature's bounty, instead of simply hustling along to who knows what and where.

People are waving and smiling. A woman pulls over and says she's seen me walking north on three consecutive days. "Thank you for what you're doing for humanity." Wow, I'm moved.

Another driver jumps out of his 4x4 and thrusts some snacks into my grateful hands. I'm touched that he's thought of my needs in a remote area where there are no shops to re-supply a hungry pilgrim. More than once I have to beg for fresh water.

At a section of road construction where a new bridge is taking shape and a one-way system is being enforced, the friendly traffic controller admits: "I don't know what to do. We've never had a hiker through here before. I'll have to check with my supervisor."

She arrives and announces that when the line of oncoming cars has passed, the truck near me will be first into the construction area. "Please follow that vehicle and walk as quickly as possible." I have a quiet chuckle. Do I look like Jamaican sprinter Usain Bolt, the fastest man on Earth?

I give it my best shot and an elderly motorist at a viewpoint says: "You're in great shape. How old are you? Sixty three? You're a kid, I'm 82!" We laugh about that.

Nature is again working her healing on me. The ocean is a magnificent azure blue and I've visited an elephant seal colony where the bulls weigh more than two tons and make a sound like a Harley revving up in a confined space; I've watched countless turkey vultures and hawks soaring overhead; I've marvelled at the blurred wings of humming birds darting from flower to flower – and now my fantasy is of catching my first glimpse of the giant Californian Condor that has come back from the brink of extinction.

I'm appreciating that so many lovely people really care about this beautiful Earth, among them unsung heroes like California State Parks official Janet Anderson, who I find sorting rubbish for recycling.

Our walking pilgrim, seen here at Esalen on the Big Sur

She loves her job and cherishes her role as a custodian.

"It's a brave new world," she declares optimistically, "and you are part of it." I thank her for caring so much about the things that really matter.

At another state park I encounter volunteer Sonia Shields who spends much of her week manning the entrance kiosk or supervising a nearby campsite. "I was an AT&T telecommunications executive at the time they were closing a number of the Californian parks," she recalls. "I had it all: the six-figure income, the power-dressing wardrobe, the Lexus and a commute of up to 100 miles a day. It was crazy and not sustainable. So my husband and I decided there must be something we could do to become part of the solution, rather than the problem."

Now she has a radically reduced carbon footprint and lives in a modest mobile home, which she parks for free in exchange for volunteering up to 35 hours a week.

Her young husband has a rare form of bone cancer and she helps care for him while his social security money pays for their food and vegetables. They've found a way and quality of life that makes sense to them.

A few hours later I meet 74-year-old cyclist Ethel MacDonald who's ridden from her home in Montana to visit friends in San Francisco. She's a social and environmental activist who's vigorously opposing a plan to mine and pipe oil from Canada through pristine areas of the US.

"My issue is justice and peace," she says, "and part of my mission is to get more people walking and hiking." Bless you Ethel!

My journey is also introducing me to inspiring communities and workshop centers, among them the Esalen Institute on the Big Sur. It is a notable centre of light that, like Findhorn, serves as a mystery school and laboratory for change and achieving the highest in human potential. It too was born in 1962 and is celebrating 50 years of personal and social transformation.

It was at Esalen in 1980 at the height of the Cold War that secret meetings were held between representatives of the so-called Super Powers, among them eventual Soviet leader Mikhail Gorbachev who is credited with the policy of glasnost.

Certainly it would be hard to imagine a more uplifting and inspiring backdrop for any thinktank; Esalen perched just off the visual feast of Highway 1 where soaring headlands and cliffs plunge precipitously into the Pacific Ocean.

Perhaps significantly this has been a meeting place for humans for thousands of years with the Esselen Indians settling here in recent centuries because of nature's obvious bounty, the site including natural hot mineral springs, a stream delivering cool clear drinking water and fertile lands from which an abundance of delicious organic fruit and vegetables are harvested.

Not surprisingly I delight in naked contemplation of life's mysteries in one of the cliff-side hot tubs, enjoying useful insights, fascinating conversations and glimpses of whales, dolphins and sea otters.

Some days later I discover another remarkable hot tub venue with a no less inspirational view of the Pacific breaking over the rocks just feet away. Who could resist the Pigeon Point Lighthouse and adjoining hostel, named after the wreck of the *Carrier Pigeon* vessel that ran aground here in 1853?

On this particular night I've been walking more than 12 hours and can find nowhere to camp alongside Highway 1 that isn't private property or regulated by *No Trespassing* signs. I stagger along exhausted, trying to jump out of the way of oncoming cars that suddenly loom out of an inky blackness compounded by a blanketing sea mist. There is no safe space between the barriers and bushes and on-coming cars and my head torch has expired after being soaked by persistent rain.

I hear a car U-turn ahead and it appears with emergency hazard lights flashing, the driver shouting: "I nearly drove into you. You must get off the road. I'll help you."

Tommy has a hybrid Toyota crammed with three surfboards and boxes of wine and insists on driving me somewhere safer. "Have you ever heard of a trail angel? That's me," he says. "Once I was in serious trouble while hiking high in the Pyrenees in France when a couple came to my rescue and now whenever I see somebody in difficulties, I stop immediately to help. It's my karma to pass it forward."

He repacks the car entirely so I can find a seat, insists that I accept packets of nuts, cranberries and a very special slab of chocolate and drives me several miles to a remote spot where I roll out my sleeping bag, finally accepting that it is some-times necessary to break the law. In the mist and dark I can't see the *No Camping* signs anyway.

I go to sleep thinking that with angels like I've been meeting we can turn this thing around and realize our grandest visions.

When the day dawns bright and clear I'm on a cliff edge overlooking a stun-ningly beautiful beach and leave the first footprints in the sand, stripping naked and washing in a cold clear stream that flows into the sea. I feel invigorated and incredibly alive.

But the best is still to come. Despite dire warnings about the dangers of black bears, mountain lions and rattlesnakes, I escape roads and traffic, hiking the leg-endary Lost Coast and sleeping alone under the stars.

Some days later I make another important tick on my Bucket List of things to do before I die, walking unhurriedly along the 32-mile Avenue of the Giants that showcases the majesty of the world's tallest trees.

The Californian redwoods are the tallest trees on Earth

Often I veer away from the road to meet a particularly magnificent tree being, fulfilling a promise made to myself decades ago to 'hug' a California redwood. I commune with many and delight in a towering presence so overwhelming that even the birds seem to speak in reverential whispers.

This inspiring Cathedral of Nature is part of what I came to California for and a perfect place for quiet reflection on my pilgrim progress. I decide I'm doing just fine.

I'm delighted at the many changes I've made and notice that I no longer hanker after material things, my wants and needs being much the same. Sure, I do experience moments when I long for the comfort of a warm and dry bed, shelter from the wind and rain, a hot meal and the loving company of family and friends. But I'm mostly amused by my predicaments and aware that any physical discomfort is self-imposed. It's about choices.

Many days are sublime and invite a continuous attitude of gratitude.

One particular entreaty has been uttered so often it's become my mantra: *'Please guide me, inspire me, and show me how I might best be of service.'* Recently, realizing that I shouldn't leave out the fun element, I added: *'Please show me how I might best be of service in ways that are joyful and sustainable.'*

I've found a real sense of purpose and know that if there is a better way, it will be revealed to me. For a while I lost my focus in my quest for speed and thrills, but now I have it back again. I'm choosing to make a difference.

Since the start of my pilgrimage I've taken more than six million steps and traversed vast landscapes – entire countries even. It has been a journey of exploration and discovery that has also resonated with others. We're all in this together.

Many know that our current ways simply aren't working: it is time for a new consciousness and a new way of being together upon the Earth.

It is time to heal our disconnection from each other and the natural world. We need to reconnect with the infinite wisdom of Nature and celebrate the miraculous interconnectedness and interdependence of all life.

All thoughts, words and actions are creative and what we focus on is what we'll get more of, so let's ensure it's on being the best that we can be.

Let's look to the heavens, knowing we are all capable of more than we dare imagine, each of us having a unique gift to bring to the world.

The challenge is to step away from the clamour of busy lives, allowing time to listen to those whispers of inner knowing that are amplified in the silence when we go within.

My hope is that you are already following your passion, or, if you haven't yet found your true purpose, that you are listening attentively for those inner cues. Perhaps it will be while walking in Nature with humility, gratitude and an open heart that the answers will be revealed.

My prayer is that we can join hands and be the changes we wish to see.

PILGRIM LESSONS AND REMEMBERINGS

- A journey starts with a single step that takes you closer to your goal
- We are all capable of much more than we imagine
- We need to dream big and understand that nothing is impossible
- It is important to always respect our intuition and inner whispers of knowing
- Sixty-something, or any age, is a number and not a limitation
- The time is always right to do what is right
- To change anything in your life change your thinking about it
- Whatever you focus on becomes your reality, so make it inspiring
- The spark of divinity resides in everyone even if it is hidden
- Each person brings a gift and we need to be a precious gift to them
- There is a lesson in every situation and event
- There are no coincidences in the universe
- There is an interconnectedness and interdependence of all things
- The most important question is: What would Love do now?

Yes, there is life after cars, 4x4s, racing and rallying

ACKNOWLEDGEMENTS

COVER PHOTOS

Geoff with Findhorn sign © Chris Brown
Geoff walking © Inga Hendriks
Geoff airborne © Alan van Rooyen

INSIDE PHOTOS

p. 97   © Deon Ebersohn
p. 181 © Doug Ellis, *www.dougellisphotography.com*
p. 134 © Friends of Peace Pilgrim
pp. 11, 110, 118 © Inga Hendriks
p. 61, 186 © Adelle Horler
p. 23 (Tammy on her wedding day) © Kate Howells
p. 126 © Michel Mulder
p. 93   © Dibash Onta
p. 103 © Greg Vogt
p. 30   © Charles Ward

All other photographs by Geoff Dalglish

I AM VERY GRATEFUL for all permissions given and would like to thank everyone who contributed to this book. If someone has accidentally not been named please contact me, so that this can be corrected in the next edition.

— GEOFF DALGLISH

WISH TO KNOW MORE ABOUT
THE FINDHORN COMMUNITY?

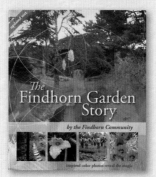

The Findhorn Garden Story by The Findhorn Community
ISBN: 978-1-84409-135-5

This new edition — for the first time with colour photographs — explores the relationship between the founders and the angelic and devic realms. At the same time it also explores the wider work of the Findhorn community and the huge effect it has upon all who visit.

The Gentleman and the Faun by R. Ogilvie Crombie (Roc)
ISBN: 978-1-84409-179-9

Follow Roc's path in *The Gentleman and the Faun* as he meets the faun Kurmos in the Royal Botanic Garden in Edinburgh, discovers the realm of the elementals and, eventually, meets the great god Pan himself. *(Only available in Europe).*

available from Findhorn Press
www.findhornpress.com

WISH TO KNOW MORE
ABOUT EILEEN CADDY?

God Spoke to Me by Eileen Caddy
ISBN: 978-0-905249-81-0

Opening Doors Within by Eileen Caddy
ISBN: 978-1-84409-108-9

Flight into Freedom and Beyond by Eileen Caddy
ISBN: 978-1-899171-64-4

Footprints on the Path by Eileen Caddy
ISBN: 978-0-905249-80-3

It is over 50 years since Eileen Caddy first received personal guidance from a 'still, small voice' inside herself, a source she called 'the God Within.' From that day on she not only lived her personal life by that inner guidance, but was also instrumental in creating the international spiritual community centred around the Findhorn Foundation in Northern Scotland.

available from Findhorn Press
www.findhornpress.com

WISH TO KNOW MORE ABOUT THE PILGRIMAGES TO SANTIAGO DE COMPOSTELA?

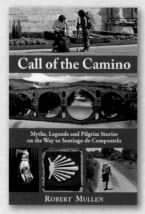

FINDHORN PRESS

Life-Changing Books

For a complete catalogue,
please contact:

Findhorn Press Ltd
117-121 High Street,
Forres IV36 1AB,
Scotland, UK

t +44 (0)1309 690582
f +44 (0)131 777 2711
e info@findhornpress.com

or consult our catalogue online
(with secure order facility) on
www.findhornpress.com

For information on the Findhorn Foundation:
www.findhorn.org